Yvonne

MEMORIES OF
The Girl from Ballygawley

MEMORIES OF
The Girl from Ballygawley

FROM FLOUR SACKS TO LINEN

Elizabeth Faulkner Praamsma
AS RECORDED BY
Peg McCarthy

TIMELINES
GENEALOGICAL RESEARCH

Copyright © 2011 Timelines Genealogical Research

All rights reserved. No part of this publication may be reproduced, stored in a retrieval system or transmitted in any form or by any means — Electronic, mechanical, photocopying, micro reproduction, recording or otherwise — without prior written permission of *Timelines Genealogical Research* and/or Elizabeth Faulkner Praamsma.

LIBRARY AND ARCHIVES CANADA CATALOGUING IN PUBLICATION

ISBN 978-0-9737809-5-6

Produced: Sharon Murphy/Timelines Genealogical Research
Edited: Carol Fordyce
Cover and text design: Tannice Goddard

Additional Copies available from:
Timelines Genealogical Research
www.timelinesresearch.com

*Dedicated to
my maternal grandmother
Elizabeth Jane Echlin McAfee,
who taught me to love the night sky,
to wonder at the stars,
to be awed by the feast of the forest,
and to appreciate afternoon tea in a fancy restaurant,
and who inspires me to keep the tradition
of making Irish soda bread.*

Contents

Preface 1

PART ONE: THE EARLY YEARS

Chapter 1: Elizabeth Faulkner 5

Chapter 2: My Father's Death 25

Chapter 3: Methodist College, Belfast 29

Chapter 4: Mother's Second Marriage 33

PART TWO: MOVING ON

Chapter 5: Canada 43

Chapter 6: New York 53

Chapter 7: The Prairies 59

Chapter 8: Graduation and Marriage 63

PART THREE: THE MINISTRY

Chapter 9: Kitchener   73

Chapter 10: Bobcaygeon   79

Chapter 11: Cobourg   81

PART FOUR: ADDITIONAL THOUGHTS

Chapter 12: Harry   87

Chapter 13: Miscellaneous Memories   93

Genealogy Reports for the Descendents   101

PREFACE

Doorways

I LOVE THE TITLE OF a favourite book of mine. It's called *Doorways in Time*. All of us have our own doorways in time.

As a child, there was a doorway that seemed to me to lead nowhere of significance. It was into a room where my father lay. It was nighttime — much past a child's bedtime. I was led through that doorway by an invisible hand.

I kissed my father very gently, and uncertainly, and I tried to say the Lord's Prayer, but I couldn't remember it. "Thy Kingdom come," and then my mind went blank. My child's mind couldn't make meaning from the words. So I tiptoed back and got under the covers of my own bed in the dark of night, lighted only by the moon.

I didn't understand why my father had died or what had caused him to die. I didn't understand that there was no such place as nowhere, or that all doorways lead to somewhere.

Another memory and I was at another doorway. Not much more than a year after my father's death, I remember a field of green grass and summer flowers and clean air, and while I wander off, perhaps to chase a butterfly, I realize the friend with my mother on that walk is a very significant person.

That evening's awareness is a doorway that will change my life, and my brother Harry's life, and my mother's life, and we all learn very quickly to love and trust this man, even as our mother loves and trusts him. And so was opened a doorway to a whole new world with this young Welsh Methodist minister who manifested a life dedicated to his ready-made family, but, above all and below all and around all, dedicated to God. His name was Aelfryn (Ivor) Ernest Jones, born in Llandudno, Wales.

Ivor took us through many doorways. For a time, during World War II, he was a chaplain to families seeking the dead, or sheltering themselves from enemy bombs in Belfast. After the war, Ivor's ministry took us to several locations in Ireland — to Kilkenny in the southeast, to Kinsale on the southwest coast near Cork, to Enniskillen on Lough Erne in Northern Ireland, and then to Belfast — going through another doorway with each move.

The 1950s was a significant decade for a large part of the western world. From the British Isles there was a massive exodus of people for the shores of North America. A spirit of newness and change was in the air. A new doorway was to open when the Cunard Lines' passenger ship, the Franconia, carried Ivor Jones and his family to Canada. We spent a year in New Brunswick, and then another doorway led us to Montreal, where Ivor and Mother lived for twenty-four years.

My own life took me through additional doorways — geographical doorways opening to New York, to Saskatchewan, and finally to various locations in Southern Ontario, and there were other doorways, like my university years, marriage, children, and many years in the ministry within the United Church of Canada.

A formal portrait with Harry.

PART ONE

The Early Years

●

I See the Moon and the Moon Sees Me ...

CHAPTER ONE

Elizabeth Faulkner Praamsma

With my mother at home in Castlegore.

I WAS BORN AT HOME, at Castlegore, County Tyrone, Ireland, with nurse Kyle in attendance, on September 9, 1933. My mother was Dorien McAfee Faulkner, born on August 14, 1911, in Quetta, in a part of India that is now Pakistan. My father, Robert (Bobbie) Faulkner, was a landowner and farmer at Castlegore. I was baptized in Castlederg Presbyterian Church.

When I was young, I walked a lot at night with my grandmother, Elizabeth Jane Echlin McAfee, and we'd look at the moon and the stars in the sky. During the war, we'd see the searchlights from Belfast and we would look for planes caught in the searchlights' beams. I'd skip along, jumping in and out of grandmother's shadow, while singing:

> *I see the moon and the moon sees me.*
> *God bless the moon and God bless me.*

The moon has remained a conscious constant in my life. I still go to the window at night and gaze at it, where it is a comforting mystery in the night sky.

My maternal grandfather, Johnston McAfee, married Elizabeth Jane Echlin (in County Wicklow, Ireland). Johnston was from England and served with the military in India. I was named after my maternal grandmother.

Dorien McAfee, my mother, was the oldest of five children. One of her siblings died and was buried in India. The grave of that child was swallowed in a subsequent earthquake, an event much grieved by my grandmother as a great indignity of planet earth. One sister, Gladys, moved to British Columbia. Brothers Freddie and George stayed in Ireland. Dorien died in Cobourg, Canada, in 2007 at the age of ninety-six.

A baby picture of my mother, Dorien McAfee.

My father, Robert Faulkner was a landowner and farmer at Castlegore, in County Tyrone. Robert (known as Bobbie) died in 1942. His sister, Margaret (Maggie) Faulkner, and brother, Samuel, never married and both died in a house fire. According to family stories, a lot of money also went up in smoke because they never trusted the bank. Scorched bills in large denominations were scattered on the lawn by the force of the fire.

My mother and my father met in an Irish hospital ward in the early 1930s. My grandmother, Elizabeth McAfee, a widowed mother, was visiting her daughter, Dorien McAfee, who was suffering with appendicitis in hospital, and a middle-aged unmarried landowner, Robert Faulkner, was visiting his middle-aged sister in the same two-bedroom hospital ward. At first my grandmother thought it was she the middle-aged man was interested in, but it

Mother's first wedding — to my father, Robert Faulkner — with Aunt Gladys and a friend, and no one looks very happy!

became obvious that the budding of a romance was between him and the young woman, my mother, who in his mind would make a good helper on the farm. He and grandmother were about the same age. My father was more than thirty years older than my mother! I don't know what kind of a relationship Mother and my father would have had with such an age difference.

I don't think that my mother ever really fell in love with Bobbie, but she saw all that went with this marriage, which was a good life material-wise — and she did have that. Mother was never a typical farmer's wife, though — she was outgoing and social. Her marriage gave her the opportunity to move up and go out to a different world. Before her marriage, she was employed for a short time as a "companion" to a lady of the local gentry. This gave Mom a taste of what life could be like, if one just had a bit of money!

Dad had horses and milking cows, but it was not a huge farm. He leased some land. The front door of our house looked away from the road and over his land and farm properties. Mother loved to garden, and she loved roses all her life. She had a beautiful garden, even at the farm. She planted daffodils all down each side of the long drive to the road — it was a real picture in springtime.

I went to live with my grandmother (Elizabeth Jane McAfee, née Echlin, called Lizzy) when my brother (Robert Henry Faulkner — Harry) was born in 1936. A nurse lived in Mother's house for a year to help Mother care for Harry. My grandmother, who was youthful for her age, loved and wanted me. I was three years old and she spoiled me rotten, and, where my mother was quite the disciplinarian and very efficient, my grandmother was more relaxed and easygoing. I never remember her being angry — she was a very serene person. My mother had a large cozy kitchen with a settee in it. Everything was meticulous. I remember once I put my feet on the settee rug and ruffled it up. She got angry and I packed my little bag and left. I walked down the road to get the bus, without a penny in my pocket. I was going to grandmother's house! Needless to say, I didn't get far.

How could my parents, my mother especially, give her little curly golden-haired girl to another caregiver — albeit a gently loving grandmother? That question always stays with me. I think it was because there were few cars then,

Harry and I with Mother, Grannie, and our nurse.

and mother did a lot of moving around on her bicycle. Mother wasn't born to be a farmer's wife who stayed at home; she did a lot of socializing, and she did it on a bicycle with a carrier for only one child. She was never welcomed into the Faulkner family, and she was born with brain cells that spoke to her about being the lady of the manor, not an extra farm hand. NO milking cows for Mom or cooking for farm hands. She bought herself a good bicycle with a carrier and a child seat and that was her escape. She could take only one child, so when Harry came along, I "temporarily" went to grandmother's house, and stayed! With two children, mother could not have got around very easily. The other side of the story is that Grandmother really didn't want me to leave her.

It's hard to imagine a child of our privileged world growing up in an unfranchised world, often unsanitized, no television, only radio, where listening to the 11 o'clock news was a big thing — listening to Churchill give his wartime pep talks in his deep reassuring voice, and then going to bed knowing everything was going to be okay.

Grannie and her bike — a favourite pastime. I love her feistiness in this photograph.

Harry and I as children.

My grandmother loved to walk, and we went for very long walks in the evening. One of our walks was along a country road, where we took a short cut over an old-fashioned stile, along a river, and through a field. We kept a watchful eye to make sure that the bull was nowhere near! We would walk to Cassie's for milk and skim the cream off the top to use in tea or to make custard — it was an idyllic existence! While Grandmother was visiting with Cassie, I was free to wander on the farm. There was an old rusted car in the yard in which I would sit for as long as I was allowed, imagining I was driving all over the world, never dreaming that one day I would own my own car. Only when Harry was visiting did I have to give up the driver's seat, which never seemed fair because he was younger. Grandmother loved to read newspapers, and when *The News of the World* arrived I would lose her for hours while she devoured it. My grandmother made delicious Irish soda bread, and she loved to have a cup of tea at any time of day!

A fairy tree (hawthorne) — A single Hawthorne tree left in a field was believed to be magical. Photo: Google image.

Right at the top of a hill at grandmother's house was a fairy tree — a blackthorn tree left alone in a field. It was a special place to sit and dream or make wishes. There was no TV, just this fairy tree on the hilltop where I'd sit and dream dreams and feel the world was a wonderful place. I wonder if the fairy tree is still there? It was very common to plow a field and leave one blackthorn tree; in fact, it was considered unlucky to cut it down. My own children grew up surrounded by city. I'm glad I had my young life in the lovely Irish countryside with all its superstitions.

The world changed so very much in my lifetime. I can't imagine what it holds for my grandchildren. Will they touch the stars, and will it be any more thrilling than the nighttime Irish sky before light pollution, or stepping along a safe rural road with its high perfect hedges, singing "I see the moon ...."

Christmases were very special when I was a child — because it was wartime and every little thing was very precious. From my twenties on the years were pretty affluent — everyone went overboard. I remember more fondly the early ones where you got an apple and an orange, and that was a big treat; the rest of the year you had to share one with three other people. I remember hanging stockings up with the apple and orange in the foot of the stocking, but I don't remember what else filled it up. I remember gathering sticks for kindling the fire in the great iron stove with its oven for baking and its top for boiling water, and its doorway for throwing out heat, and exposing the stories to be read in the hot coals.

I always remember Grandmother's hair in a bun — she never changed it. At night she would undo the bun and her hair would flow over her shoulders. It went white when she was very young, after the birth of her last child. My grandmother's husband, Johnston McAfee, was killed in the First World War when a torpedo hit his ship. That was when her hair turned white. She was widowed with four children — Uncle Freddie, Uncle Georgie, Aunt Gladys, and Mother (Dorien).

Uncle Freddie's friend, Sam Elliot, visited grandmother's every Thursday night and each night put a shiny half crown (two shillings and sixpence) in my moneybox; that bought a lot of candy in those days, but Grannie made sure I put a goodly share in the post office savings account. All the years of my early childhood that money accumulated in that account and finally went into "half-crown heaven" — 10 years' worth. I went to boarding school, grandmother eventually died; and who knows what happened to the contents of my moneybox savings.

Grandmother with Mother, Uncle Freddie, and Uncle Georgie. She was a widow on a widow's pension, with four children, but she was always the lady.

My uncle Freddie, who really was like a father to me, built me a wooden house in the garden. The princess's dollhouse was in the news at the time, and I was Uncle Freddie's little princess. He built me a house you could stand up in and I had my own fenced-in garden. My grandmother would come and have tea in "the house" — probably water or juice! It had shelves with china on them, all provided by Uncle Freddie. He gave me my first real watch that you wind; I was careful not to lose it, and I had it for years. Uncle Freddie lived with Grandmother until the end. He never married. I have always qualified my Irishness as being

Northern Irish — in other words, I'm under the queen — a monarchist? No, not really; but as a young person I was enchanted by the princesses, as everyone was — Princess Elizabeth and Princess Margaret.

Me with Grannie in her garden.

Me with Uncle Freddie in Grannie's garden.

I have never seen such a huge holly tree as the one at Grandmother's. It was much admired by many for its enormous size, its health, its shiny prickly leaves, and its red clustered berries. It was the one tree we didn't befriend as children.

I bicycled miles to piano lessons through hail, rain, and snow. Cycling was the only way I got there, and my grandmother insisted that I learn to play the piano. In my senior years, I'm so glad of that early discipline. To sit and doodle on the piano is my number one therapy — as long as my fingers work.

Grandmother loved shoes and I remember getting X-rays of my feet in shoe stores as she shopped for footwear. It was a terrible thing, but it made sure the shoe fit correctly. You stood on this machine and it showed your bones. I used to stand and look at my toes. I realize now that's where I got my shoe fantasy — I have more shoes than I can ever wear. They got rid of the X-ray machines pretty quickly when they realized they were dangerous.

I suppose for most children — in city or forest, on mountaintop or prairie plain — there are forbidden and forbidding places. It was no different in my childhood place. There was a lake, small by Irish standards and a puddle by American standards. My grandmother's second house, across the road from the first, had originally, many years previously, been the main gate lodge to an estate. Now it was just a house on its own half-acre or so with a lovely stand of trees across the driveway, and beyond those tall trees and down a sloping hillside was the lake, owned by the Erskine family who farmed from their home across the lake — a large grey house with about eight large windows from which to view the property. It was all a very tempting playground, but forbidden. The story that this was a bottomless lake was believed, so don't dare try paddling your feet in it, and there were monsters in there that must never be disturbed. It worked. Nobody ever went near that lake. Even the cattle in the fields stayed well away! They drank from troughs laid out in strategic places.

Me with Grannie in her garden.

Me with Mother in our garden.

Rivers are a memorable part of my life — especially at Grandmother's, but also when I lived along the Miramichi River in New Brunswick, and the St. Lawrence in Montreal. The river of my childhood was flanked by hazelnut trees whose branches in season were loaded with nuts. I'd sit on the river's banks and watch the pools and eddies. "The river" is the only name my childhood river ever had for the locals, and it flowed and rippled over polished rock and stone. "I'm going to the river" was a frequent childhood saying, and I'd be off to gather stones or nuts and just to paddle around.

Farmers rode their horses and carts over the river, and pedestrians and cyclists used the wooden pedestrian bridge that spanned the shallow waters on one side and the suddenly deep dark pools on the other side — the scary side, the "don't go near" side.

It was near this river I had a frightening wartime experience. Frequently I would go to the river through fields, but occasionally I would go by a dirt road. One day I went by the fields but came back by the road. You had to climb a hill and then make a sharp turn, and, as I came up the hill to the top, I saw that the embankment had crumbled and, when I looked over the edge, there was a military tank on manoeuvres that had taken the turn too sharply; the ground had given away and the soldiers had been decapitated. This accident was still at its rawest, still warm state. It was my most awful memory of the war — the blood and the helmets and the bodies lying forlorn, somebody's sons, husbands, lovers, or friends.

Seeing that turned-over tank was a rare picture of the war in my experience, but that horrible scene was etched in my head forever; for a long time after I couldn't go on that road. The powers that be didn't clean the scene up very well, and scattered pieces of paper and metal remained for a long time. Who were those men? And what were the messages on those pieces of paper? It was the only time I ever felt real fear, a "scared to death" feeling, and yet it was not a scene that gave me nightmares because I heard stories of the war on a daily basis. I did not linger over the discovery of the recently overturned army tank at the bottom of an embankment. It was an unlikely scene of war where cattle grazed and primroses grew and a young girl was out for an otherwise uneventful trip to the river.

As for wartime experience, that was my only moment of lost innocence, though I did pick up on some anxiety from grandmother. On our evening walks we would watch for the searchlights, and I knew they were looking for enemy planes. Those must have been gruesome days, but my memory of the war is mainly pastoral. I experienced great drama — the night skies lit

Uncle Freddie during World War II, 1943.

up with beams of light that seemed to touch the very edge of heaven, new people, new children, evacuees come to live in another land, time when even children became silent while adults hung on every word of Winston Churchill at 11 o'clock every night on the radio. They were comforted by the sound of his voice and his reassuring words, and we went to bed knowing everything would turn out all right. There were pictures in The News of the World of bombed homes — street after street. There was rationing of food and clothing, but we never wanted for anything. My grandmother frequently made champ — potatoes mashed up with really creamy

Uncle Freddie during World War II, 1944.

milk and eggs and onion tails — and we had chickens. Grandmother always had a dozen laying hens. I know they were spoiled hens, in the sense that we spoil our pets. They had all the comforts of their special henhouse — a choice of heights on which to roost, and a choice of nests in which to lay their eggs. The nests, about eight of them, were in a row of boxes, the right size for each hen to feel comfortable! But despite their creature comforts, you never knew when one of them would end up in the soup pot.

A picture taken by Uncle Freddie of a mountain in Darjeeling in 1940.

A picture of Mount Everest taken by Uncle Freddie in 1940, during the war.

The waste nothing ethic was a way of life entrenched in my childhood and stayed with me forever. World War II meant rationing, smuggling butter, limited sugar ... and clothing coupons. We made dishtowels from flour sacks. Because there were shortages of staples, my grandmother had a skirt that was designed to hide precious blocks of butter inside it that she could smuggle over the border from Ireland (Eire). She loved lots of butter on everything. When we crossed and the custom officials would ask "anything to declare?" My grandmother would say, "no — just visiting." During the war even the less privileged had a plot of land for vegetables, chickens, a large garden, and apple trees, and stored potatoes and turnip in clay pits, and it never seemed that we did without.

Uncle Freddie in World War II – he is the one holding the hatchet.

I remember gas masks, and the ones for children weren't properly fitted. I never had to use one, but they were scary looking things. During wartime, I went with Grandmother to a school to "choose an evacuee" — there were all these little children, far from home, and you had to choose one. The English girl my grandmother chose had lovely red hair and she was sad. I can't remember her name, but she lived with us for about a year. With no comprehension of the trauma this child must have endured, I just saw her as a new friend. At night she joined grandmother and me on our nightly walks.

We loved the darkness of the country roads, lit only by the light of the moon. Grandmother would tell us stories about the man in the moon. Belfast was still being bombed, and sometimes the searchlights that streaked the sky would pick up a warplane. We never talked about whether it was friendly or German, or whether it had dropped a bomb on an innocent family in Belfast, or whether it was on its way to drop a bomb on a family in enemy territory.

Uncle Freddie in 1943.

Uncle Freddie in 1944.

None of the Faulkners but three of the McAfees voluntarily went to war — Aunt Gladys, Uncle Freddie, and Uncle Georgie, who abandoned his platoon. Mother got a telegram from the war office saying George McAfee was missing, presumed dead. He had deserted (a crime), but for some reason he never paid a price for it. He was an artist — really a lovely artist — and not cut out to be a soldier. I wish I had his self-portrait that hung on Grandmother's wall. I loved the blue, triple-folded letters they wrote, always telling me to be a good girl and look after Grannie. Georgie would write me letters, and each airmail envelope had a strip of his art across the top. His handwriting was a work of art with capital letters curlicued and enlarged as if each sentence would be of memorable interest and importance. I was sheltered from any fear Grannie felt for two sons and a daughter in uniform.

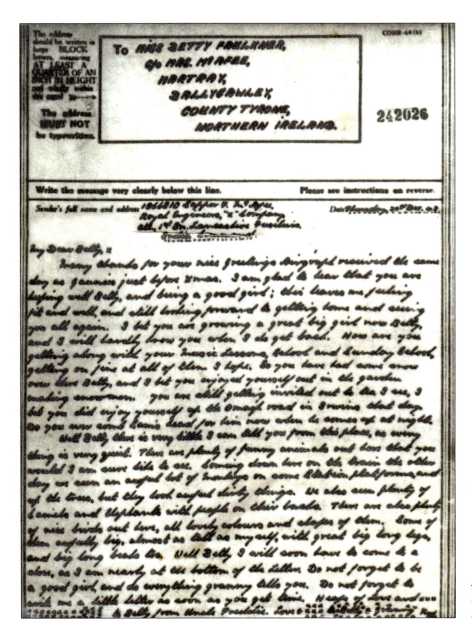

A letter uncle Freddie wrote during the war.

In another memory I'm in Crossley's Plantan (plantation). There's a carpet of bluebells at my feet, and trees with arms outstretched inviting me and my younger brother to climb high, higher – then Harry falls. Harry is two-and-a-half years younger than I and so I'm responsible for him even though I'm only about 10 or 11 years old.

I can't remember the details of what follows, but Harry fell off a branch and chopped his tender young tongue with teeth not yet blunted with age — blood flowed and I was terrified. I next remember sitting on a bus. How strange the infrequent Dungannon/Ballygawley bus should come along just then. We had no money, but the bus driver took us aboard and dropped us off in the village at the doctor's house. Harry probably hadn't a potentially severed tongue but it seemed like that to me, his "big sister." But I think of that occasion and wonder at the simplicity and trust that got two children out of a scrap without health cards, or an appointment or even money for the bus ride. We had to walk the mile home from the doctor's house.

A "cut-out" picture of Harry and me.

I remember refusing to recite a poem at a Presbyterian Church Sunday school concert; the poem was "When I grow up I'm going to be a soldier." I was told later I started the poem and quickly stopped and said, "No, I'm not going to be a soldier." Maybe I was eight years old and I did not know then that in the future I would stand up and sing "Onward Christian Soldiers," though I suspect the poem was about a soldier in the early 1940s.

My first love at ten years of age was Freddy Hopper, yes, Freddy Hopper!! My second love was at age thirteen; Alec Leslie was sixteen. They say you never

Alec Leslie, my second boyfriend.

forget your first love and I haven't forgotten him but I don't feel the presence or even see the face of that person. In contrast, my second love still makes time stand still for me. I remember the magic of our first kiss under a lamppost in a quiet street in Cork. Alec went to cadet college for a career in the military, but he left without permission, and because he had deserted, he could never leave the south of Ireland.

I will remember forever stealing a ten-shilling note from Grandmother's purse. I went to the candy store — old-fashioned, with rows of candy jars — and bought a few pennies worth of candy, and I got all this change and I didn't know what to do with it — oh, the guilt!! So, what to do? And I can't remember how all that worked out, but I do remember I hid the nine shillings and sixpence worth of change in my playhouse for some time, and eventually I had to "fess up."

I went to a two-room schoolhouse when living with Grandmother — I guess I was a bit favoured because the teacher, Mr. Robb, had two boys, Derek and Jim, one older and one younger than I, and we were like family — those two boys were my playmates. I didn't have any girlfriends in the early years. Master Robb was really good to me, maybe because I lived with my grandmother. I was at their house frequently, which was three to four miles away. It was all very innocent — playing, climbing fences, running along riverbanks, skipping stones.

My grandmother read the coals in the fire. We burned either coal or turf, and my grandmother's "seeing things" fascinated me. It was a rural superstition to predict all kinds of things from the kinds of holes made by the fire. In particular, I remember a kind of clear hole that burned fast and looked like a cave; it would eventually collapse. I remember she said, "There's going to be a death in the family," and within five weeks of her saying that, which was not that long, my father died — but she probably knew he was ill. You didn't often see those kinds of holes and it always meant something bad was going to happen — like a death.

I remember Grandmother was dramatic about it, and the fire holes were the clearest in her new Rayburn range — it was the cat's whiskers! She had this old black iron range with the oven on the side for years, and then she got the

With my Grandmother when I was about 10 years old and in my Methody uniform.

Rayburn. It was yellow with chrome and had a great oven. It burned well and left really clear holes. It had a hot water tank in the side, and a large oven because she loved making bread. I also went with her for teacup readings. We'd go miles to Dungannon to get her cup read. One day the woman said Grandmother would soon be standing on church steps, and a short time later my mother said she was going to get remarried, so that reinforced the old superstitions.

There was no magic in the cup or the tea. The cup could be made of the finest china, fragile in the hand, or it could be as sturdy as a working man's mug. The magic was in the leaves, good broad tea leaves scooped loose into the pot. When brewed sufficiently, the copper-coloured tea was poured, but the purpose was not to enjoy the aroma of jasmine or the taste

Uncle Freddie, in his hand is his pipe.

of orange pekoe grown at five thousand feet and therefore without bitterness, the purpose was to drink the cup empty, leaving the tea leaves clinging to the sides and bottom like stranded minnows, and the teacup reader would place the cup upside down on its saucer, turning it three times. Then the fortune teller had the magic map to import the promise of the future to the eager customer.

Another negative superstition was seeing a lone black crow or a hole in the clouds — that meant something bad was going to happen — and then, of course, the opposite — a four-leaf clover meant good luck was coming one's way.

CHAPTER TWO

My Father's Death

I HAD OFFICIATED AT THE burial of dogs, cats, and butterflies on many somber occasions during the first decade of learning about life. They were solemn ceremonies with no lasting consequences, no significant tears, no questions, and no guilt. Puppies, kittens, and butterflies were always in abundant supply, in barns, woodsheds, and meadows. Despite the ready supply, a new one always brought its share of excitement, assuring the buried one was soon forgotten. But those experiences didn't prepare my childish self for the death and burial of a real human being; people had always seemed so invincible.

It was difficult when Bobbie, my father, died. He was tall and lanky, with a stern, unsmiling face. Maybe it's the wedding picture I'm remembering; nobody is smiling in the wedding picture — not the bride, not the groom. I wondered why the bride would get all dressed up in fancy clothes and carry flowers and a little purse hardly big enough to hold the penny you might use for the lavatory.

When Bobbie died, I was quickly prepared for the funeral (that meant Sunday best clothes and a toothbrush in my little case). You see, Bobbie's house was not my house. I was living with my grandmother, two towns away—two buses away—too far away in those days for frequent trips. This was a journey to the house where I was born, a journey to say farewell to my father. Those were the days before funeral parlours, embalming, and satin pillows.

Bobbie was laid out in the spare room at the top of the stairs, across from the bedroom he had shared with my mother. The door to that room was closed, but I knew where Bobby was laid out. I suppose I was told I mustn't go there!

I don't remember feeling sad or afraid, just some sense that this was a major life event, or death event — or both. Nobody sat me down to tell me about life and death.

So it was that my child's mind turned to the Lord's Prayer to make some sense of the events around me. I said it every night at bedtime; it was as much a part of my life as cleaning my teeth or skipping rope. When all was quiet and sleep had taken over an exhausted household, I decided God needed to know about this child of His who had died. With the power of my secret rendezvous with God and father, I tiptoed in the stillness of the night to my father's death room and knelt by his deathbed and spoke in whispers my prayer. Halfway through my mind blanked, and I felt afraid for the first time. The words wouldn't come, and I wondered if God would forgive me. I crept quickly back to my own room, so tired.

The next thing I remember is the hearse moving slowly down the long lane the next day, turning right at the gates, the black ribbon proceeding to I knew not where. I just knew it was not a place where women went. We huddled together and watched the men, young and old, black as crows, following the black hearse, which was pulled by two black horses. Bobbie my father was dead, remembered as the only witness to the night I forgot the Lord's Prayer.

The point of this is that I spent a period of my life as a United Church minister in fear that I would forget the Lord's Prayer, and I couldn't leave home without a copy with me. It was written out all over the place — in the Bible, under the pulpit, in wedding and funeral service books.

My parent's house had been big enough to have boarders — it was a large farmhouse — so they offered their home to a series of ministers who came to work in the area. Ministers were moved around a lot. One time my parents boarded a Presbyterian minister (Reverend Lyons) who killed my mother's roses because he would go out at night and pee on them. That always bothered my mother. When my mother remarried after father's death, it was to one of those young ministers who had boarded in our home.

My mother Dorien McAfee.

My early life was a collision of worlds — the house where I was born, the fields, the rocks, the streams, lakes and rivers of Ballygawley and Castlegore, contrasted with boarding-school life in Belfast. My life was a mixture of rural and urban — old and new world Ireland. Ireland was a class conscious society; the gentry class was declining but still felt — they had their own pews in church. Estate owners still had gatehouses and governesses to educate their children.

I keep looking for a thread of constancy in my life, and I know, when we write about our lives, it's neither lying nor truth-telling. We give thanks for a life lived, and often do so because there is a sense of thankfulness for life at its various stages — but the stages are not like gift boxes of individual size and colour. The boxes of life can't be juggled into various positions, some discarded and some treasured. The boxes of life are chaptered into overlapping stories to be explored.

My field hockey team at Methody boarding school in Belfast. I am second from the right in the top row.

Methody headmaster Mr. Falconer with me sitting on the ground.

CHAPTER THREE

Methodist College, Belfast

At the age of ten I went to Methody, a boarding school in Belfast. This was a huge change from my easygoing life with Grandmother and familiar faces and trusted strangers, to time alone with new faces — more new faces than the population of the village of Ballygawley. Large hotels and streetcars and huge educational institutions and museums were now my immediate world. I think of this in contrast to my grandmother's environment, which was landscaped against the lake and the hill and the rural road to Cassie's farm for milk.

I was at Methody for three years, from 1943 to 1946, and I loved the environment and the new experiences. I fell in love with my Latin teacher, Mr. Drennan. I loved Latin because of him, and to this day I can still conjugate a number of Latin verbs. I played field hockey — sometimes goalie and sometimes right wing, but mostly centre forward.

A huge highlight was the regular visits by Uncle Freddie who would make a long bus trip every Sunday just to take me to high tea. We would sit in the front row of a double-decker bus and go to Bangor, a seaside resort, and have high tea by a window. I never realized until much later what an effort he made for me. I loved him.

My field hockey team at Methody.

With friends at Methody.

Three images of me in my school uniform at Methody.

The headmistress of Methody was stony-faced Mrs. Rose. She had a large, cold office that intimidated me, and it's where I ended up when I was reprimanded for sneaking down the back staircase to go outside for some soil. My aunt had given me bulbs for potting, but I had no soil. The school was very strict, but I decided to climb down the fire escape and steal some soil one night, and I was caught red-handed. My mother was notified, too. I wasn't a rebel kid, but Mom was pretty furious.

Train travel during my Methody years was exciting. You could open the window and fix it open with leather straps and put your head out, making sure the smoke wasn't coming your way. It was smoke you didn't wish to inhale as the lumbering monster huffed and puffed across the countryside. The rhythm of the engine and the song of the whistle were far more exciting than any amusement park. How trusting everyone was — the porter would watch out for me — as I'd travel from north to south to visit my family.

Mother and Harry shopping in Cork — a favourite pastime.

CHAPTER FOUR

Mother's Second Marriage

M OTHER REMARRIED IN 1944. Her second marriage brought her a whole new life. She married a young, recently ordained, good-looking Methodist minister who was an amazing Welsh tenor soloist. His voice gave you goosebumps. His name was Aelfryn Ernest Jones and we called him Ivor. He had boarded in my mother's house when he was doing student pastoral work.

He would take my mother through risk and security, through laughter and tears, on a honeymoon in wartorn London as naturally as he would take her on a surprise bicycle ride in rural Ireland. There was love and laughter,

Mother and Ivor Jones in 1944.

Postcard of Kinsale, a seaside town my parents lived in for a while.

fear and hope, amidst the dust of the last days of World War II bombings. For a time, he was a chaplain to families seeking the dead or sheltering themselves from enemy bombs in Belfast.

After the war, Ivor's ministry was offered in tranquil and lovely places in Ireland, and especially in making a home my mother often recalled — in particular, a tiny dream house nestled at the foot of Kilkenny Castle. From the castle to the Atlantic Ocean (Kinsale) to Lough Erne (Enniskillen) and then to Belfast, he brought us all through a doorway in life that was very much centred on the church, and full of liveliness, fun, and song, that occasionally made Mother wonder if she would see another day.

I remember when my mother and my stepfather were wed. I remember the outfit I wore — a soft wool green coat, the colour of grass shoots, with a narrow black velvet collar and black buttons. It was a beautiful coat, and I had black patent leather shoes to match. I felt like one of the princesses in the glossy royal family magazines every good Northern Irish citizen subscribed to. It seemed like every Roman Catholic family home had its little red candle burning beneath a picture of the Virgin Mary, and every Protestant home had its picture of the King and his family, including the corgis. Whoever we were, there was someone to watch over us! — and the Protestant kids could dream of becoming princesses.

I had never been to a wedding, and little did I know this one would turn my life upside down and back up again. I was really impressed with this man that Mom was marrying. My father had been a really elderly man in not good health, which gave him a severe unsmiling countenance. Mother's new husband, Ivor, was young, full of fun and tricks, and offered a whole new future.

Mother with Ivor's first car after they were married.

To the wedding my grandmother (mother of the bride) wore black! And even my young mind wondered if this marriage was fuel for gossip and legal wrangling. Without a doubt, the locals believed this handsome young man could better have taken the hand of one of their eligible daughters, but instead he chose the challenge of a fashion-conscious young widow and her two children.

The prim and ever so proper Presbyterian clan of the Faulkners (my paternal family), the backbone of the Presbyterian Church and outstanding citizens in their community, were set to claim their rights and those, they believed, included the guardianship of Bobbie's children, especially the male heir and chattels. The first item of business for my mother was the hiring of a good lawyer, and without a worry she planned her future. She won her children and property rights, but she left no friends among her in-laws. Her future became financially secure — not the usual fate of most young widows barely over thirty years of age.

And so, in style, Mother in her dusty pink wedding dress and I in my lovely green coat and Grandmother in black and a dozen or so others, mother married this dashing young Welshman who hadn't a penny to his name, but had started his career with a voice from heaven, good looks, charm, and a wake of disappointed young women.

Harry and I lived with Grandmother while Mom and Ivor took off for London on their honeymoon. It was the worst year of the bombing, and they spent their first night in a bomb shelter — what a way to spend your honeymoon! They said they were going to visit friends, but came back with stories of sirens, scrambling in the middle of the night to air-raid shelters, huddling together like frightened animals, while London came crashing down.

While I was in Methody, my parents — my mother and stepfather — moved to Kilkenny. They lived in a most adorable small row of houses at the base of the ancient Kilkenny Castle. It was really an upscale bachelor condo that was transformed from the former castle stables.

Mother and stepfather Ivor with their dog, Rickie, at their home in 1946.

My stepfather was moved around a lot because he was a Methodist minister. After Kilkenny, they moved to Kinsale, where there was freedom to explore forest, river, and dungeons. Today's parents would have railed off the cliffs because the waves were huge, but we seemed to have had the sense to know our surroundings. It was a most beautiful place to live, and my mother thought she had the world by the tail at that point. They lived overlooking the wild Atlantic Ocean, and they did the most foolish things. I was about thirteen, but even at that young age I thought how irresponsible they were. Once when I was visiting from Methody they had gone out in a rowboat on the Atlantic Ocean. Kinsale had a very sheltered harbor, but once out of the narrow opening you were out in the wild Atlantic. This time they had to be rescued when wind and waves became dangerous.

Mother and stepfather Pappa Ivor in their stables-converted home at the foot of Kilkenny Castle in 1946.

It's a trusting wife who heads into the roll of the Atlantic Ocean in a rowboat. No matter how much she trusts the man with the oars, being in a row boat that suddenly seems bound for the United States of America, or a watery deep, tests one's trust. On one occasion my stepfather nearly didn't make it back. Mom was watching from the window and that must have been really scary. All the houses in this seaside town were stacked on a hillside; nearly everyone had a telescope, and the whole village must have been aware of this crazy person out in a boat.

It's a trusting wife who takes the turns on an Irish country road on the back of a motorcycle not the driver's own. But Mom found she was always safe with Ivor. His life of family and professional ministry was intertwined and filled with friendships and variety; the joy he found in preaching and in singing and in conducting missions was the same joy he found in comforting or celebrating with others. His tenor voice charmed many audiences, as when he was guest soloist for special musical events, such as The Messiah or The Crucifixion, in a cathedral setting or in a small, rural church.

Heathburn Hall was a popular picnic place for our family. This photograph was taken in 1950.

The time in Kinsale and our yearly holidays at the seaside further sealed my love of ocean waters. It's hard to believe how one could have been so content in such a simple time. Where will we go for a holiday? Bundoran? Or Portrush? They were our only options in the whole world, but they were the world and they were wonderful and we weren't even thinking of options. Now, when I stand before the long list of tour destinations at the local travel agent's window, all I want is a piece of rocky shore, with some good Atlantic Ocean, with spray crashing prankishly in every direction over screaming children racing, but failing to stay dry, and braver less agile souls just melting into nirvana surrounded by the sounds and touch of nature that forever stay in memory.

With Harry in Glengarriff, public gardens in County Cork.

My first encounter with racial issues was when a student, a lovely brown-skinned young man, perhaps from India, began to visit my family. He was eighteen or nineteen and I was fourteen — and we were becoming conscious of each other. Local families were encouraged to invite young foreign students into their homes because these students were often far from home. This young man visited a couple of times, and then, because we were starting to become interested in each other, which was an absolute no-no because of skin colour, the visits were ended.

Harry and I in a hothouse in the south of Ireland in 1950.

At home in Belfast with our dog, Rickie.

Christmas in Belfast — Collecting money for Dr. Bernardo's homes, with a friend.

My cousin Josephine and I, the picture of innocence, playing around a haystack.

My cousin Josephine, around the age of ten, and a friend.

PART TWO

Moving On

I See the Moon and the Moon Sees Me ...

CHAPTER FIVE

Canada

In 1954 we made the trip to Canada on the old Franconia — the same ship on which Churchill signed war documents. My mother wasn't too excited about coming to Canada, but said she would try it for a year or two. It was a time of mass migration, and many of my stepfather's friends were leaving Ireland, partly because the system of the church was freer in Canada. In Ireland, Methodist ministers had to move every three to five years.

A little of our furniture was getting shipped to Canada, including Irish linens. Mr. White of White's china store in Belfast gave mother a Royal Doulton figurine to take with her. She put it in a hatbox with hats under it and over it to keep it secure. I can still see her walking proudly onto the old Franconia through the crowd with the hatbox on top of her

A postcard of The Franconia.

head. She looked crazy, but it was to protect her figurine, which was a treasure to her. Because my stepfather was a minister, we got treated extra well on the ship, and one of the perks was the privilege of sitting at the purser's table.

Harry, Mother, Ivor, and me on the deck of The Franconia, 1954.

Mother and Ivor on the deck of The Franconia, 1954.

Quebec City was the arrival place of new dry land in 1954, and Dad's ministry with the United Church of Canada began with a year in New Brunswick followed by nearly twenty-five years in Montreal. He seemed to work harder than ever as he became immersed in the Canadian church, but he still found time to include family in travel to many lovely places across Canada and Europe, and time for new friends. There were evenings of story sharing, some around the piano, and old-fashioned games, and in 1967 he even found himself with an invitation to Buckingham Palace for tea in the garden, and he took great joy in taking my mother to meet the Queen.

Our grand Belfast home at 26 Wellington Park — in contrast to the one we moved to in New Brunswick that shook every time a train passed.

When we were preparing to leave Ireland for Canada, stepfather Ivor told us we were going to a place close to Darby Junction. In Ireland, anything that was connected to a junction meant it was a hub of activity and a significant and sizeable place. When we reached Canada, we were greeted by several people in different vehicles. We thought we were going to somewhere big. But then we passed Darby Junction. We saw an old, fallen-down sign saying "Darby Junction." It hung by a single nail at an abandoned railway station where the weeds and the grass had overgrown the tracks. It was a moment of letdown, to say the least!

However, we really were fortunate. Most immigrants took up land and worked hard, but my family landed in clover. We were received with open arms, with a house and community in New Brunswick on the banks of the Miramichi River, and a guaranteed salary. Dad had a three-point charge. We arrived in July 1954,

"The house that shook" and our first car in Canada, 1954.

and my birthday was September 21. No one had a twenty-first birthday like mine. I had a three-tiered cake, and my mother sent to Ireland for decorative symbols because a twenty-first was a big deal. The whole community came to the party and I didn't know anyone. I got all kinds of presents — cups and saucers galore. It was a huge party. The cake decorations were damaged on their way across the Atlantic Ocean, but we managed to assemble them on the cake. Over 150 people came, and I didn't know one of them. Later on I took some of the cups and saucers back to the only store they could have come from and traded them for jewellery or something like that.

My 21st birthday party in New Brunswick. (Note the cutout of Harry and me on the table behind.)

Mother and me at my 21st birthday party in New Brunswick.

I wrote about living on the river:

> *The Miramichi flowed wide and unruffled*
> *Deep to its bank and deep to its bed*
> *Cradled timber floated lazily in the sun*
> *Until somewhere a house or a boat or maybe an outhouse*
> *Gave new form to wet forest wood*

We lived in this old wooden house across from the river close to the railway tracks. Mom would straighten the pictures every morning and twice through the day because the trains would shake the house as they rattled by. It was very different from the prestigious home she had left at 26 Wellington Park in Belfast. At first she wouldn't even unpack. We had a big pot-bellied stove with exposed pipes that went up and into the ceiling. You'd be freezing and would stand against the pipes in your pyjamas to get warm. It certainly wasn't what Mom thought Canada would be.

But I loved that snowy year. The ice was so thick on the river, we'd skate around bonfires. Mom bought her first skates. She always thought that if you paid more for something it would be better, whether it's clothes, cars, or skates. I always picture my mother with the best of things. This time, she

Skating near our home in New Brunswick — Mother in her street coat and skates.

didn't realize the skates were more expensive because they were figure skates. She couldn't move forward at all, and she had to get the picks

Wrapped in bear skins, going through the forest in New Brunswick.

Horse sleighing in New Brunswick.

Me with my cross-country skis in New Brunswick, 1954.

filed off. It became a joke in the family that whenever she wanted something we'd say, "Just make sure it doesn't have picks on it."

It was an amazing year and I'll never forget it — shad fishing, going in sleighs pulled by horses through the forest with bear rugs to keep us warm, snow to the chimney tops. You drove and all you would see was the smoke and the chimneys and part of the roof — but roads were cleared well enough for safe driving.

Mom had a boat for fishing and one day she went out with her rod. The fishermen were up river catching shad in nets; she rowed up to where they were fishing, and the men gave her a shad. She rowed back down and, when she got off the boat, she had this big fish. She had a weird sense of humour. There were a few people around who jokingly asked if she had caught it, and she said, "Of course I did!" The story got into the paper — "Minister's wife the first to catch shad on a line."

Hunters (friends) in New Brunswick, 1954. I am far left and Ivor is on the far right.

Ivor and friends with killed deer, New Brunswisk, 1954.

Fishing with Mother on the Miramichi River in New Brunswick, 1954.

We had a party-line telephone with more than twenty families accessing it. When you'd get a call, you'd hear all the phones clicking on and off and hear people knitting as they listened in on the calls, or you could hear the radio in the background. Everyone had a different number of rings, and the minister's phone was a popular number to listen in on!

I worked in the Royal Bank in Newcastle and drove every day with this man who had lost his arm above the elbow. He drove a huge car. At first I thought he should not be driving, but his car was adapted to his prosthesis, and it turned out just fine.

We stayed in Millerton for eleven months before moving to Montreal in 1955. The move was a big jump. Mom and Dad stayed in Montreal for twenty-four years and Mom loved it, especially the shopping. I got a job, then went back to school at Concordia (then, Sir George Williams) and McGill — and got my degrees. I took my Bachelor of Arts and then my Bachelor of Divinity, finally graduating in my early thirties, having worked through some of those years.

The roads after Hurricane Hazel in New Brunswick in 1954.

Mom was the hostess with the mostest — an amazing hostess! Some of her linen tablecloths and linen napkins were incredible — with the finest crochet on the corners by women from Connemara — and now they sit yellowing in my drawers. The Montreal Symphony Orchestra quartet was a regular guest at our evening church services. Ivor was a Welsh tenor soloist and through his singing, made friends with the orchestra members. We would sing around the piano at our house after every service. That was beautiful. We lived at 1254 Beatty Avenue. Mom was a great baker and she would serve her much appreciated sponge cakes with whipped cream, cookies stacked with butter cream, raspberry preserves, and the silver tea pot — she was so elegant and she didn't know whom I took after! Sadly, her legacy didn't live on in her daughter — unless I really try.

There was a special quality and joy in all the doorways Ivor Jones went through, and that special gift was his gift of singing. From tenor leads in the oratories at an Irish cathedral to the soft song of prayer at an old person's bedside, God gifted him greatly and gifted others as they listened to him.

While we lived in Montreal, we took some trips home to Ireland, and on one of them we visited France. While there we stayed in a wine grower's chateau within a hop and a skip from the palace of Versailles. Louis Collard, a cheese agent from France, and a very handsome, suave organist at Verdun United (in Montreal), became a family friend. He had a reclusive wife back in Paris, who, according to Louis, lived in a Paris apartment and wore cashmere! At our disposal while at the Carmichael chateau were three Citroen automobiles, and a toot of the horn on exit or entrance signalled an almost invisible gatekeeper to open the gates. Dinner was in a huge dining room — with the family and my parents and me seated at this highway of polished mahogany that was not conducive to feeling relaxed. Neither was the offer of wine, since water

Ivor and me in 1954.

During one of our semi-annual trips home to Ireland when I was in my early twenties, we visited friends in Versailles and stayed at this wonderful villa.

would have been normal for my family — my step-dad was a teetotaller. Here we were with no milk, no juice, and no water — just wine, and any choice, it seemed, from a wine cellar like an underground city! Even the teenagers had a 'Doesn't everybody do it?' kind of comfort.

In my twenties, I worked for a Montreal ship-broker and, when he moved to New York, I didn't. I stayed and worked for IATA (International Air Transport Association), which I did not enjoy because my new boss's ethics were not the same as mine. I learned I had to travel with the boss, and there were expectations of me. I didn't stay very long when I discovered what my first assignment might be. They only hired young, pretty girls. Luckily I got a phone call around then from my old boss, asking if I would consider coming to New York. I went right away. It was the best thing I ever did.

CHAPTER SIX

New York

When I moved to wonderful Brooklyn, New York, I worked in Manhattan. I had an amazing boss and wonderful friends. Those were great years. I worked for World Bulk Shipping Ltd. at 26 Broadway Avenue, and went back every summer to my old desk during the seven years I was in university programs. It was special for me to be assisted in this way as I took my degree programs. Here I was, studying for the Christian ministry, and being helped in so many ways by my Jewish boss.

In New York, I would go to Broadway shows and do all kinds of things together with my friends on the weekends. Jones Beach on Long Island was a summer favourite. Every Saturday I explored Manhattan one street at a time. There was every nationality and every economic status. I loved to window shop and cash shop, to go into the churches with their beautiful architecture and their inner sanctuaries, with the quietness a wonderful contrast to the outside world. I loved the pace of the city. I remember writing a little poem about a pigeon in Greenwich Village. It was a very quiet street and there was a pigeon there. It stirred something inside me.

```
A LONELY PIDGEON


A bird upon a sidewalk
A pidgeon, in the heat of the noon-day sun
Without movement, unheeding of passers by
Perhaps it thought, too, upon the hardness of human hearts.


There was shade by the walls of the jail
There were men inside with hearts to love a bird
Unafraid of disease ... what disease ... they say birds carry disease
But the jail-birds were behind the stone walls.


Was its wing broken ... no, it didn't look like that
Or perhaps a leg
Maybe it just felt sick to its stomach
Birds do get sick - don't they


The sun got swallowed up in the line between earth and sky
The sidewalk cooled for that great hot mass had ceased to burn
The jail still stood and the men inside
But the bird ... how ... where ... who
Did it gather strength ... did it struggle to live
Did it have the help of a gentle human hand


It was not there ... then where ...
```

A poem I wrote one day after walking through Greenwich Village.

The first coffee shop that I was aware of was a chain store called Choc'Full of Nuts, and when I found it I thought I'd died and gone to heaven. I could take a break, drink good coffee, and read the newspaper, all for the price of a cup of coffee! My love of reading newspapers was inherited from grandmother who religiously read 'The News of the World'. I still love to read The Globe and Mail in a local coffee shop. Coffee and newspapers have been forever linked, "You can't have one without the other."

My old boss, Elie Schalit, invited me back to New York, to my old desk and old role as his right-hand woman, every summer after I returned to university in Montreal. He was a practising Jew who helped to put a Protestant young woman through divinity school. There is surely a powerful sermon in that act of crossing religious boundaries.

While in New York, I decided that I wanted to learn to dance; as a Methodist young person, that had never been part of my life. I considered myself to have "Methodist feet"! At Arthur Murray Dance Studio, I took the bull by the horns in an attempt to learn how to dance. I really enjoyed dancing, but had to have a strong partner. My instructor could lead me in the cha-cha and the tango with the greatest of ease. My parents knew nothing of this. A youth dance was organized at my church in Brooklyn and my Arthur Murray instructor said he'd go with me. Wow! I was going to dazzle my friends there because I was going to do the cha-cha and the tango and wow them all, but who walked in — unexpectedly, uninvited, and unwelcome — my mother from Montreal! She didn't tell me she was coming. The Georges, who ministered at the church, were friends of my parents and told them about the dance. Mother came to scout out whom I was with. I have never forgotten seeing her walk in and my feeling of guilt, because I knew her perception of the Arthur Murray Studio. But I did a good job dancing and she was impressed with that: she would sometimes turn up unexpectedly, and loved doing that — she was a free spirit, not because she was necessarily checking up on me, but because she liked the surprise element!

Friends in New York who were my family when I lived and worked there. Third from the left on the top row was Max Mobley — a serious boyfriend — a young Methodist minister on Long Island.

I had a good friend called Bill Mowat who was an assistant minister at Hausen Place in Brooklyn, and we were part of a group who went to shows and the beach and generally socialized together. He was a friend of my parents, too. I wanted to buy him a present, something that made a statement. I wasn't in love, I just thought he was a great guy and I wanted to tell him. What could I get that was special? I went to Fifth Avenue to Tiffany's, no less, and I remember well looking over my shoulder and feeling completely out of place. The doorman in his uniform ushered me through the great brass door. I was looking for the cheapest thing I could find so I could have it in a Tiffany's blue bag. I found a tiny little tie stud that probably cost more than I wanted to spend. I asked Bill for the bag back and I still have the Tiffany bag. Needless to say, it is somewhat faded and shabby looking.

Heroes in my late twenties and thirties were John Vanier and Richie Bartells. Vanier inspired me through his books and, in particular, his public service in his role as governor general. Richie was the most fun young guy and part of our gang in Brooklyn. He was so crippled from polio, and yet survived it with such a spirit of leadership and thankfulness for his life.

My parents and I went back every other year to Ireland, mostly by Cunard ship, which became our favourite way to travel. The ships became more and more lavish, but none had the charm of the old Franconia. On the Franconia the five days would be spent creating entertainment for the passengers and everyone got involved. We made some good friends and had a lot of fun doing skits and telling stories and jokes. On one of those visits, back home, while shopping in Belfast, I saw this brilliant yellow rain hat, fashioned like a felt hat with a lovely black-bound brim that turned up. I bought it, and I thought it was one of the nicest hats I ever had. Since it was pouring rain, I wore it to church at Grandmother's in Ballygawley. I discovered when the service was over that the price tag, large as life, was still on. I was so embarrassed I didn't want to go back to that church for a long time, knowing I would be remembered for "the hat."

In 1956 during a trip back to Ireland, I went to the Echlin farm, having decided I wanted a three-legged milking stool. The farmer said he would make me one and asked how many cows I had back home! He made me an Irish milking stool and he even left it in the barn over night to make it authentic. Back in Canada, the customs official asked me if I had milking cows in Montreal. The Echlin's were cousins of my mother.

After travelling by boat over many years, we started flying across the

> Have just got orders from Switcher to
> bring he to Dungannon for little present for Betty
> Will have to go.
>
> Sept. 18th 62
>
> My Dear Dorrie —
>
> Your letter rec yesterday glad to hear from yous. An what a surprise yous me to know I had forgotten Bettys Birthday. the first time in all her (life) till her im sending her a small present an I hope she had a Happy Birthday an hope she will forgive me. did I tell yous a lovely pigion came to us has been with us for some weeks. this morn I looked out an there were 2 a lovely white ours is grey an Red legs Walter was up on Sunday evg an I was thinking of going to Baptist Church to hear Norman Porter preach, I could not go our service on Sunday is at 4 o c an there are to be 3 ministers Rev Brooks an Presbyterian Rev Porter Smith from Belfast Baptist an our own I may go, no word word of the Rectory been Built) love to all next space yous Fred love from XX
> by order   Mother

A letter from Grannie with a note from Uncle Freddie.

Atlantic. Flying has changed since those trips back home. In those days, you dressed up to travel. We used to fly Aer Lingus and always got free drinks of choice and sample bottles to take home. The meals were so good that once I asked for the recipe. It was for lobster crepes and they mailed the recipe to me. I still have it. Now you're lucky if you get a sandwich wrapped in plastic.

We used to go camping and those camping trips were with a canvas tent with a pole in the centre. Mom and Dad liked to camp, but in a "let's live

Embroidering a tablecloth.

with an equipped kitchen" way. We took so much stuff — like proper pots and pans. We would go to New Jersey or the Maine coast and I just loved that. I remember leaving with all these pots and pans tied to the roof rack, and now I think we must have looked like gypsies. After I married, my husband, Peter, and I and our two children continued the family tradition of camping. In later years, my parents would come along so we'd have six in the car and a dog and all our camping equipment.

I remember designing a new Canadian flag and sending it to Prime Minister John Diefenbaker in the 1960s just before Expo 67. I wasn't one for getting involved in political stuff but I decided I would send Diefenbaker my flag suggestion. I went to a lot of trouble and I sent it off and I think I got a little thank-you note back. I thought mine was really good. It was an interesting exercise designing something to represent your whole country. The maple leaf doesn't represent all of Canada. My flag, at the very least, had a great highway weave across land from east to west.

Naomi and Andrew on holiday in Cape Cod. We loved camping in the United States.

CHAPTER SEVEN

The Prairies

I TRAVELLED TO SASKATCHEWAN DURING my post-graduate program to a Pastoral charge with three small churches. While I was a student minister there, I lived in a little wooden house in a place called Compeer, 100 miles west of Saskatoon, close to the Alberta border. It was prairie heaven. There was nothing but skies and wheat fields. The night skies felt like a brilliant canopy of glittering lights that was beyond words, demanding awe. I remember the village with the grocery store, and pub, and my outhouse — people who got drunk at night, especially Saturday nights, would come over and, uninvited, use my outhouse. I recall that was an unpleasant part of life in Compeer. The toilet was a "public" outhouse, the bathtub was an aluminum tub that hung on the wall, the clothes drier was a line strung between two trees.

Nearby there was "Charlie's garden." I will never ever forget Charlie. He was deaf as a doornail but would come to church every Sunday — he couldn't hear a thing, but he loved the feel of being in that worshipping community. He grew vegetables and donated his crops to a school for orphan children. He grew flowers just for the love of them. I was supplied with armloads of gladioli. I loved Charlie. He had two shacks — one for him and one for his mother.

My little house in Compeer, Saskatchewan, where I was a student minister in my late twenties.

His was a mess with cans of open food everywhere, and flies! You didn't even want to have a cup of tea there, but I closed my eyes and had tea. His deceased mother's house, across the yard, was a different picture. It was immaculate with not even one spider web. Charlie had a sweet personality. He wrote to me for years and I wish I'd saved the letters, with his perfect handwriting and homespun philosophy about life.

The one and only time I drove a tractor was on a prairie wheat field. The tractor was easier to drive than the ancient car supplied to me for the summer. The car had a rubber tire attached to the floor, to hold my stick shift in the right place. It wasn't meant for muddy gumbo roads with gophers popping up everywhere. One time a fellow student at another charge and I decided we'd like to go to British Columbia to see the Rockies. We met at the edge of the mountain range for our journey. I took that old car to our meeting place and I prayed nothing would happen, for I was far beyond our local boundaries. The car and I both made it home.

Another time I took the car for a preaching service some distance from home. I travelled back late under a beautiful starry sky. What I had hoped

My trip to the Rockies with a friend in my not-so-roadworthy car.

wouldn't happen — did. The car broke down. All I had was a bag of buns, Barney my dog, and my Bible. I could hear wolves in the distance. Eventually a car came along and stopped. I wasn't at all afraid, but I'm sure these people were wondering why this young woman was all alone, late at night, far from anywhere. We left my car on the roadside, and they took me home. It turned out they were from a place close to my hometown in Ireland! We sat up talking to the wee hours, so they stayed the night! The old car was retrieved by someone on the Pastoral charge and I was reminded it was only for *local* travel!

Prairie storms were beautiful, with their massive lightning strikes, crackling through the clouds and splitting the landscape. I remember the fear when camping in Saskatchewan, during lightning storms. The steel tent poles were lightning targets. I lived with Grandmother's fear of electric storms. She spoke of destructive thunderstorms when living in India. She would tell me to get into the darkest corner, away from windows. In our tent, there were no windows to move away from, neither were there dark corners!

As a student, I served a pastoral charge in Baldwin Mills in the Eastern Townships of Quebec. It was a place peacefully nestled in hills and on a lake, surrounded by families considered to be the salt of the earth. It was an unsettling time. I was learning how complicated people are with their private and public personas. To my left, my trusted neighbour was not to be trusted. To my right, a stalwart citizen, the "salt" of Baldwin Mills, punished his young daughter by locking her in a wardrobe in a room I temporarily rented in his house. Back then, of course, no one reported family abuse. They were a prominent family who lived on a big farm, in a house on a hill that overlooked the village. I was afraid, and without disclosing too much, I was able to move to a lovely cottage.

> *Memory is the cabinet of imagination,*
> *the treasury of reason, the registry of conscience,*
> *and the council chamber of thought.*
> — WRITTEN BY A FRIEND ON THE FRONT PAGE
> OF A PHOTO ALBUM, DATED 1964

CHAPTER EIGHT

Graduation and Marriage

Petrus (Peter) Praamsma was a Dutchman who was in the same class during my Bachelor of Divinity program. I was the only woman in my class and, when Peter and I got engaged, I was the only female at the bridal shower! One of my male classmates dressed up as a woman, complete with a long train that ferried my gifts! The local newspaper got involved because we were "a couple," graduating together from Divinity School at McGill; rare in the '60s but not such a rare thing anymore.

I was thirty-four and, to my parents' dismay, I got married instead of ordained. Peter and I wed on October 28, 1967, in Verdun United Church, Quebec, and then went to Gagnon, Northern Quebec.

We bought a new car that was transported to Gagnon by train because there were no roads through the Quebec wilderness to the town. It was a great year, even though there wasn't a lot to do socially. The community had a lot of alcoholism and tragedy — horrible stories, like one about a child who froze to death in the cab of a truck while her parents were drinking in a bar. There was an Olympic swimming pool that no one used. The black flies were horrendous. While we had a washing machine and a dryer, I was the only

Divinity Graduates, Clipping from The Montreal Star.

Divinity Graduates, Clipping from The Montreal Star.

GRADUATION AND MARRIAGE

Our wedding shower, where I was the only female because my divinity class was all men (except me).

Cutting the cake at our shower.

Our formal wedding portrait.

Peter and I with Mother on our wedding day.

Peter Praamsma and I married on October 28, 1967, in Verdun United Church, Quebec.

crazy fool who preferred to use a clothesline. The sheets were so frozen they would crack coming through the door — but they smelled lovely!

As the minister's family in this ore-mining outpost, we were somewhat special and we had the luxury of using the company plane to go back and forth to Montreal. The president of the company — the one industry in town (iron ore) — belonged to our church.

While in Gagnon, we adopted a child, Naomi Dorien Praamsma, who was born July 4, 1968, and who came to our family in August. She had her first airplane flight at six weeks of age. Her birth parents met at Expo '67 in Mon-

GRADUATION AND MARRIAGE

treal. An English Montrealer (mother) and an Italian (father) representing his pavilion met and fell in love. Naomi was born with flashing dark eyes — surely her Italian father's!

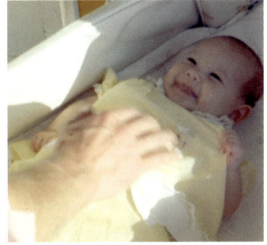

Naomi in Northern Quebec.

From Gagnon, we moved to a three-point pastoral charge in the village of Fitzroy Harbour, on the south side of the Ottawa River northwest of Ottawa. We lived in an old two-storey wooden house with a potbelly heater that never seemed to warm things up (unless you sat on it).

Andrew, our son, was born in Ottawa Civic Hospital on June 16, 1971. He gave short notice of his arrival into the world. It was late in the evening, I was having labour pains and there was a seventeen-mile drive to the hospital. I had a real sense of urgency. We got into the car, Peter turned the car key to leave, then turned it off and went into the house to get a banana in case he got hungry!! Priorities! I remember thinking, "Well,

A typical Christmas morning — Andrew and his beloved teddy. Mother mended it several times.

The family is introduced at a new charge.

there's a snack bar at the hospital," and that is almost the only thing I recall about the arrival of Andrew.

In 1981, while on vacation in Maine with my mother and Papa Ivor (that's what Naomi had called him when she had trouble saying Grandpa) wearily in his wheelchair, and scruffy Andrew as a child, and my little dog, and an orange picnic cooler, and it's the end of a long day of travelling, and we need a place to sleep! We arrived at this fancy hotel in Rochester with a gorgeous lobby. We were so exhausted from driving that we booked a room for the night rather than find a campsite. The hotel was very grand, and it felt odd to have arrived with our camping gear while all these smartly dressed guests milled around. But there we were in camping clothes with dancing partners and late-night dinner guests in tuxedos moving around us. We got a grand room, and ordered top-rate food to our room and had a luxurious bath, and paid as if we were eccentric millionaires!!

Then we got a call from Naomi in Ottawa saying that

A family portrait

GRADUATION AND MARRIAGE

Naomi and Andrew making a design with yarn, or perhaps playing cat's cradle.

Andrew loved to draw, and this is one of his sketches made while on holiday in Cape Cod in 1980.

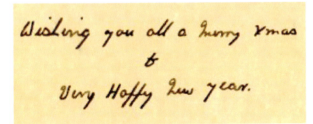

A Christmas note from Uncle Freddie in 1975 in his impeccible handwriting..

Uncle Freddie was ill. Mom and Dad flew to Ireland immediately, and I felt deeply saddened that I couldn't immediately go to my favourite uncle's funeral. My dear Uncle Freddie was gone, and I never told him how much I loved him.

Peter and I divorced in Ottawa when the children were thirteen and ten. By then I was ministering in a pastoral charge part-time. One night I came home around eleven o'clock from a church meeting. The children were tucked in bed and fast asleep. A note lay on the kitchen table. It said, "I am future oriented — I will be in touch. Peter." The very next day I purchased a top quality small cooking pot — a small one so that I could use it to cook for just myself when the children were with Peter — in 2011 it's still my most used saucepan! It cost me a fortune, but it lasted me forever!

PART THREE

The Ministry

I See the Moon and the Moon Sees Me...

CHAPTER NINE

Kitchener

LIFE AS A WOMAN minister in the United Church of Canada was still breaking new ground. Old ways and expectations die slowly. It was a man's world in the Church in the '60s — I had been the only female in my class during my theological studies. Now it's a woman's world, at least in the United Church of Canada. In the early years when I was ministering, I overheard part of a conversation at a new parish, "She's a good minister; it's a pity she's a woman." That spoke volumes about the struggle with acceptance. It sounds unbelieveable in 2011, but I caused waves when I preached *without a hat* in a Montreal church in the 1960s; there was a flyer written about it and placed in everyone's mailbox in Verdun. It was printed by a fundamentalist element that believed a woman's place was not in the pulpit, and it added insult to injury to do it hatless. "For isn't it God's design that a woman's head be covered?" it stated.

I moved to Kitchener, not long after I had been ordained. I was forty-eight years old — obviously a second career! To my surprise I was called to a well-established congregation, which put me through three interviews. (We've got to be sure about this woman!) It was almost unheard of for a woman to get a

THE GIRL FROM BALLYGAWLEY

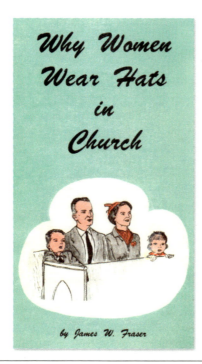

This leaflet was printed and distributed in Verdun, Quebec, about women who did not wear hats in church, particularly those who preached (i.e., me). I thought it was good because it shook things up.

Why Women Wear Hats in Church

When only a boy, an incident occurred in our home which relates to this very subject. One of Mother's special friends paid her a visit, and before leaving, they had afternoon tea together. When the visitor had gone, I asked, "Is that woman a Christian?"

Mother answered, "Yes, she is a good Christian, but why do you ask?"

I replied, "She ate with her hat on!"

It was then that Mother explained to me it was permissible for women to eat with their hats on, because that is how they are to be dressed when they attend Church and partake of the Lord's Supper. But she added, "For a man to sit in Church or eat with his hat on is not a Christian thing to do."

In I Cor. 11: 2-16, we have some expressions which are difficult to explain. Yet, in spite of admitted perlexities, Bible expositors are agreed that it teaches that men attending Church services are to remove their hats and women are to wear a head covering. In this portion we are given three reasons why Christian women are to have their heads covered with a veil or hat when worshipping in Christian assemblies. This instruction is considered important because it is linked with the ordinance of the Lord's Supper, vs. 17-34, and is, therefore, incumbent on every Christian generation, regardless of styles and changes in custom.

I. Women Wear a Head Covering in Church Because of Their Subjection to God, and Teaching of the Scriptures.

We are all under divine authority. In this Scripture men are represented as being in subjection to Christ, and women as being in subjection to godly men! The woman in the creation sense is not superior to man, because Adam was first formed, then Eve. A woman is to be subject to her Christian husband and to Church leaders if she would live in the will of God. And yet there is a sense in which she is equal with the man, for in Christ, there is neither male nor female. But it is too bad that some men still cling to the mediaeval ideas of a woman's place in life. The Scriptures do not teach that women were to be kept in bondage to men! She was never intended by God to be a slave to a man's pleasures. Her place is that of a help-meet, a companion and comforter; to share in her husband's responsibilities, sorrows and joys.

It was Christianity that brought about the emancipation of women! It is God's plan that man and wife are to be *"heirs together of the grace of life."* When a woman usurps authority over men in the Church, she is immediately out of the will of God. Public leadership in the Church was never given to women. All the apostles, pastors and teachers in the early Church were men.

An unveiled or hatless woman in a worship service is a display of irreverence to, or ignorance of, the divine plan. The heathen women were unveiled or hatless when they worshipped their gods in ancient times. But the Apostles exhorted the Christian women at Corinth and elsewhere to veil their heads when worshipping the Lord.

A few days ago I was shocked to learn of a young woman, a candidate for the ministry, who lead the Sunday morning worship service in the sanctuary of the Church, and preached the sermon, without any type of head covering. How very dishonouring to God and His Word!

Some time ago I sat through several police court sessions. I observed that all the females had their heads covered in some way. A few came in hatless, but when they realized it, they left the courtroom and returned wearing a head covering. Recently a Montreal judge ordered all hatless women to leave or be charged with contempt of court.

II. Women Wear a Head Covering at Church Services, Because it was the Teaching of the Apostolate and the Custom of the Churches.

"If any would contend to the contrary, we (the apostles) have no such custom, neither do the churches of God" (I Cor. 11:16, Lit. Trans.).

Across the years there have been a few who objected to women having to wear a head covering at Church services. Also, they have sought to confuse the message of this Scripture portion by saying that the headdress is the woman's hair and not the veil. But verse 6 makes it clear that the hair is not the head covering, or the veil that is mentioned — *"For if a woman will not wear a head covering, then she should cut off her hair too: but if it be disgraceful for a woman to have her head shorn or shaven, let her cover her head."* (Amplified New Testament.)

Recently I attended a Bible Conference where they observed the Lord's Supper at the Sunday morning worship service. I was deeply grieved to notice that of about one hundred women who were present, only three had their heads covered!

Why do Christian women follow this unscriptural and worldly trend? It is disobedience to the spirit and teaching of the Word of God! Godly women who have the moral courage to wear a head covering at such services are becoming fewer. A woman refusing to wear a head covering at Church services is, in the final analysis, displaying insubordination, not to men, but to God!

At a large Church wedding recently, I was pleased to observe that every female wore a hat. Why? I would suppose that it

Women wear hats!

Woman United Church minister plans a 'feminist' ministry

By John Asling
Record staff

When Rev. Elizabeth Praamsma is inducted as the minister of Highland Road United Church in Kitchener Tuesday, she will be making a little bit of history.

She is believed to be the first ordained woman United Church minister to head a congregation in Kitchener-Waterloo. There have been several women who have served as assistants over the years.

Praamsma, a native of Ireland, comes from Ottawa where she has served in an Anglican-United joint congregation. She graduated from McGill University in Montreal in 1967, a time when there were few models for women in ministry.

While the situation has improved since then, Praamsma said Highland Road is still doing a little pioneering by hiring her. "They've done by choice what the church will have to do down the road five years from now."

"More than 50 per cent of new graduates are women. You can't just send them all to the bushes anymore, there just aren't enough bushes," she said in an interview this week.

Asked if her ministry would be feminist in nature, she replied, "I hope so. I think the male ministers who have been appreciated the most in congregations have feminist qualities."

And she indicated that some of the traditional housekeeping concerns of women help make her ministry effective, anything from making sure there are flowers for the sanctuary to making sure that structures work well.

She also feels that women may have an edge in the caring and nurturing skills that are needed in counselling and one-on-one ministry. "I'm not an academic," she said.

While studying at McGill she was the only female in her class and was honored by being named the top preacher in her second year. Since that time she says preaching has been a joy and a challenge.

"On what other occasion can a person address so many people at one time?, she asks. "The responsibility to bring the Christian message tests our willingness and strength to be God's person."

Praamsma will be inducted by Rev. Bob Duthie of Cambridge, chairman of the Waterloo Presbytery of the church at 7:30 p.m. Tuesday at the Highland Road Church.

She has actually been serving the church since July when she replaced Rev. Larry Wiegand who is now minister of a congregation in Bobcaygeon.

Feminist minister: Newspaper clipping from Kitchener days.

senior ministry position in a city church at that time in the Church's history. Usually women got a small multi-point charge or worked as assistants. I previously did weekend supply work. The move was a risky step for the congregation, and they wanted to be sure I could preach as well as a man! They came twice to Ottawa to hear me, after interviewing twelve people, and not one of them female.

I stayed at Highland Road United Church for twelve years, bought my own house, and made wonderful friends. Andrew made best friends there also, but Naomi never adjusted well to the move. Ottawa was where she wanted to be. She made herself an apartment in the basement during her rebellious years. I later discovered the basement window had made a handy exit for her nights out. My neighbour pointed out how the grass beneath the window was well trampled down!!

The twelve years of ministry at Highland Road was my longest stay in one pastoral charge and, as I was their first woman minister, the whole ministry was a bit of a barrier breaker. I officiated at a wedding one Saturday and, when one of the men was making a speech at the reception, he made a reference to my personalized licence plates. They read "Ms Rev" — then he paused and added "Yours to Discover" (which, of course, refers to Ontario)! I didn't know whether to be embarrassed at his innuendo, or laugh or cry, but it brought the house down!

One of the perks of my job was officiating at weddings, and I became known for doing really personal weddings, before that was popular. I sometimes had several in one day. I enjoyed meeting the people. I'd always get invited to the reception and that was fine — no dinner to cook and I loved to dance! I once did a wedding in a hot air balloon and I was almost blown out as it landed! It was in the evening, and you had to land before sundown because the air currents change; the only place we could land without horses or cattle in the field was in rough thorny terrain. We had lost time trying to find a place. The winds had changed and the whole basket and balloon tipped over; I couldn't get out because my knee got caught, I was stuck! And there's always fear that there will be a fire from the flame.

I spoke at a women's conference while in Kitchener. It was an honour for me to speak at one of the first women's international days. The experience was a good one and led to other such invitations.

After twenty-four years in Montreal, Mom and Dad had moved to Hamilton and then to Kitchener. Dad's Parkinson's had taken Mother and the rest of the family through another doorway that was to lead us all into a different kind of understanding and living when Dad experienced the first signs of Parkinson's and, some years later, lost his sight. This doorway was to the place of surrender, to a different understanding of life's meaning and joys, and to experiencing the faith of Pappa Ivor that nothing could separate him from the love of God — not physical immobility or blindness or even the loss of speech that had previously flowed so eloquently and powerfully. The singing from his heart stayed with him through all the last difficult years. He sang when spoken words wouldn't come, and he had all the hymns written in his heart and close to his lips at any time.

In his last year of life he sang to the nurses at Kitchener Waterloo Hospital, but soon he was too sick to sing, and finally his last gift was surrendered, but I know it was in the surrendering of his last gift that he heard Christ sing the words he himself often sang as Christ's ambassador "And because I live, you too shall live."

Christ's words of assurance led Ivor Jones through his last doorway, this time to watch and pray over us. There is no such place as nowhere. My mother, my brother Harry, and I myself had richer lives because of the influence of Ivor Jones. In the words of Shakespeare, which he loved so well, "Good night sweet prince and may flights of angels sing thee to thy rest." A door had

MY OWN CHURCH

> To Dorrie—
>
> Just a piece of paper, a pen and a heart filled with love - for you must know it already - I love you.
>
> I love you for being just you, my wife and my sweetheart. You will never know what you have and do mean to me.
>
> Often, when I have been in great straights you have helped me to be strong.
>
> Often - I have been directed by your wonderful insights and your resources of wisdom.
>
> You are not gushy emotionately — but in a hundred and one different ways, you have told me of your love for me.
>
> Please, go on understanding me and loving me.
>
> You are to me like the shadow of a leafy tree.
>
> You are to me like the music of the ocean on a dreamy day, & the trembling of music enticed by the hand of a master.
>
> These things you are to me — and more and more and more.
>
> Thank you, darling, I'll do my best to help you have the greatest Christmas yet. All my love. Ivor.

A beautiful letter written by Ivor to Dorrie.

closed, but another door opened. Mother, and my family, and Harry and his family would remember Ivor Jones and his influence on our lives.

CHAPTER TEN

Bobcaygeon

I EVENTUALLY MOVED TO BOBCAYGEON in 1992 and lived there for three years. Naomi was on her own by then, living in Ottawa and enjoying her freedom. Andrew was studying at Wilfrid Laurier University in Waterloo. I served at Trinity United Church. The ministry was part of an experiment in team ministry to a large congregation. Hiring a woman in a leadership role was still considered a bit "dicey," so the team was a new idea to serve a growing community. A black man from Zambia, Elijah Lumbama, was hired as the other team member. The "woman-black" team was a whole new ball game. The hiring committee thought it would be a great education for the community, but all around it was a bad fit.

The congregation was very polarized. The new arrangement worked for the influx of Liberal Toronto retirees — who bought homes in Port 32, a stylish housing development — but it didn't work for the rural older generation. The Toronto people thought two ministers, this team with no senior person, would be a good education for a white, male-oriented community. However, the old guard didn't approve of a woman [in the pulpit], and neither were they too open to the second minister from Zambia. The dreams for change didn't work out. Both Elijah and I decided life was too short for constant tensions. We both resigned and they didn't hire a black man or a woman again. After their three-year experiment, the church went back to "how it used to be."

This experience was also my financial disaster. I had bought a brand new house there, and when I sold it I lost big time. But it opened another doorway — into retirement. I retired early, moving to Cobourg.

I used to read my dreams, which were often very dramatic. Around this time, I had one that I took very seriously. It was a horrible dream of a wildebeest, which can get a disease where a worm gets into its brain and the wildebeest can only walk round and round in circles. I dreamt I was a wildebeest. I never forgot that recurring nightmare. I tried to make sense of it, for I felt strongly that the dream was sent with a message. I realized that, even though I could have stayed in Bobcaygeon, there was one man who had a lot of power and who would rather have seen a man in my position. I related that to where I was and what was going on, and that dream helped me to make the decision to move. That's when I retired from Bobcaygeon and decided to move to Cobourg.

It was an all-around good decision that enabled me to have the remaining years of work and retirement in a beautiful community on Lake Ontario. At first, I was busy with supply work, six- or nine-month jobs all over the area, in Trinity, Cobourg, Hastings, Port Hope, Brighton — all United Churches. I made many good friends in my new life.

I quickly found Monk's Cove, which became my favourite place for contemplation. High above the water, under a tree, I could watch the sun set with its glorious brilliant orange red and listen to the water lap the stones below. Sometimes I thought I could burst with gratitude, knowing such quiet and serene beauty far beyond anything found scrolling endless TV channels.

CHAPTER ELEVEN

Cobourg

As the years passed my mother and I became more like sisters, and towards the end the roles were almost reversed. My mother spent the last five years of her life across the road from me in Legion Village, a seniors' residence/retirement home in Cobourg.

I remember one Canada Day we went to 66 King, a favourite coffee shop. Mother was about ninety at the time. We sat in the window so we would have a good view of the fireworks. About fifty other people were there that night. I lost my handbag just before the fireworks were due to begin. I panicked and everyone started looking for the handbag, heads to the ground! As you might guess, we all missed the fireworks! I felt awful. The handbag was found at the first table we had sat at, then we moved to get a better view.

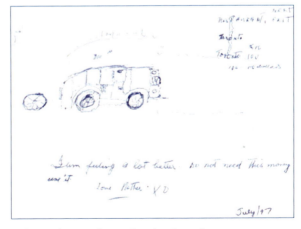

A funny drawing by Mother that I saved.

On February 18, 2007, twelve years after I moved to Cobourg, Mother died in the Cobourg hospital. I presented the eulogy at her Woodland Cemetery graveside on February 21. Part of it follows:

Those of us who were close to my mother know that she lived life as if it would last forever. She never saw herself as getting old, but I also saw signs that in her own quiet place and time she befriended death. It was alone in her comfortable chair that she sorted through keepsakes and personal treasures like notes, photographs and small momentoes. It was alone that she put those treasures in a hardback cover and wrote 'Bury this with me.' It was alone that she revisited those treasures, and, with a change of heart and a strong hand, drew a stroke through the original instructions. She was befriending death and knew her memories would be our memories and in them she would live among us.

"*Some of us will also remember her lovely rose garden in Montreal. We also remember the long, difficult time of caring for Pappa Ivor. There was also her enjoyment of silly fun, which sometimes got her into trouble. We recall her sense of style and her sometimes assertive way of living, as if she was Queen for a Day. Even at ninety-five, when she had left The Landmark nursing home for the hospital, the administrator told us she could not believe the number of men asking about mom — she never lost the ability to flirt!*

Her ability to look on tempest and be never shaken.
                                            WILLIAM SHAKESPEARE

That sums her up. My mother was a gifted woman, resilient, an excellent cook, with a wonderful fashion sense and a sense of humour.

After the service I had a letter from my son, Andrew, in which he said, in part:

Maybe I should put in writing, though, how well you did on Wednesday. The service for Pappa Dorrie [that's what her grandchildren called my mother] was a meaningful one, and you kept it appropriately simple and honest, and gave us a chance to say goodbye in a way that would have been so much colder and detached had you not done it yourself. I'm sure it helped you to have a task, but it was still so strong and brave of you to lead us in our collective farewell to Pappa Dorrie. She would have been so proud of you. I could picture her at the back, nudging one of the cemetery ladies, saying, 'That's MY daughter.' Maybe Pappa Dorrie did depend too much on Pappa Ivor and on you for her sense of who she was, but I can't really fault her for being so proud of you. I'll talk with you soon.

Love, Andrew

Mother and I in her Montreal garden the day Harry married Muriel.

Recently I watched crows building a nest across the street. I watched their diligent progression from the first gathering of twigs. I got no housework done for a couple of months. Seeing the life of two crows, building their nest and how they worked together, was an incredible experience. Then, when all was ready for family, the female would sit while the eggs were hatching and the male would bring her food. Finally, the birds hatched and, one by one, sat on the edge of the nest before flying off. One day, one stood seemingly forever on the edge and it wouldn't fly away. The mother would come and talk to it but there it stood, on the edge of the nest. Since it wouldn't fly, and after many days, she walked it down the trunk of the tree, hopping from branch to branch when possible, then jumping to the bottom. The young crow stood at the tree base for a while, then walked over to an evergreen tree and stayed for two days while the mother constantly brought food. I think it had a broken wing and couldn't fly. It was amazing how the mother looked after it. Finally mother and child walked up the street and over the parking lot and I never saw them again, but it was an unforgettable experience of how intelligent crows are.

One day a man whom I knew from Bobcaygeon came to visit me. He was very wealthy. His wife had died and I had officiated at the burial. I remember his little feet and his highly polished shoes, and his perfect shirt and tie as he sat in my livingroom. He arrived with an armload of red roses and an 18-karat gold bracelet that had belonged to his deceased wife. He knelt and placed the bracelet on my arm. I was flabbergasted and didn't know how to respond! He wanted to thank me, he said. He died soon after.

How did I ever get from there to here? From wartime clothing stalls to Saks Fifth Avenue? From reciting a poem in a concert in an Irish village to preaching a sermon in a cathedral in Brooklyn? From a two-room schoolhouse to McGill University? From wartime flour sacks to linen tea towels — I never saw my life opening up like that, and now can only marvel at the contrasts.

What foundations have guided my life? I share one … an old Methodist minister friend of Pappa Ivor once said to me, "I love to look in expensive store windows and see all the things I CAN DO WITHOUT." I never forgot that. I still love to look, and see what I can do without. I know I wouldn't have those thoughts if he hadn't impressed me about life's values.

What have I learned about life? A realization about being a part of a world "family" web where I unthinkingly absorbed so much from others in unexpected places, both the good and the bad — the yin and yang of life. It took all these decades to learn there are no second chances and the saying, "you make your bed — you lie in it," is true.

This girl from Ballygawley with her share of peace and gratitude has run a good race. I wasn't in it to win — it was enough to have shared the experience.

PART FOUR

Additional Thoughts

I See the Moon and the Moon Sees Me ...

CHAPTER TWELVE

Harry

I WISH HARRY WAS ALIVE now — I really do. I spent two-thirds of my childhood apart from my brother! How could that have happened? But when he was born I went to live with my grandmother while my mother had some time with a new baby. "Sometime" can seem like a lifetime to a child. And so it was that at Grannie's I stayed and got total attention. I never remember ever being scolded by her. Harry stayed at home in Castlegore until the remarriage of mother in 1944.

That remarriage upset the whole Faulkner family's apple cart. Now a large segment of Faulkner property would go on the auction block. It had been assumed Harry would grow up, marry a local girl, and maintain the land, but Mom took the money and made a new life with her new love. Neither Harry nor I would see or have communication with the Faulkners ever again. So sad, but Mom had never been welcomed into the Faulkner family. She was born with ideas other than farm wife in her brain — lady of the manor, perhaps. Mother was not going to be a farm hand, or cook for the "help". She bought herself a bicycle with a good carrier and child seat and that was her escape, with first me, and then Harry, on the back. Off she would go for the

Harry and I growing up.

Harry loved to ride.

Harry in County Cork — He loved horses, and that's one reason he joined the RCMP (Mounties).

Harry and Ivor shovelling snow in New Brunswick, 1954.

whole afternoon or evening visiting a cousin who was an Anglican minister's wife, or dropping in on neighbours for tea!

In 1944, Harry came for a while to live at Grandmother's because Mom's new husband got posted to Kilkenny, and later to the opposite end of the Irish isle, at Kinsale. I think that was hard on Harry. He was only about eight years old and had been the centre of his mom's attention, and now his sister resented his intrusion upon her world. He must have missed Mother dreadfully and must have been much conflicted. I remember feeling that my relationship with my grandmother was intruded upon. My grandmother must have been a saintly woman, to love whoever came under her wing — me, Harry, our cousin Josephine (Uncle Georgie's daughter), an evacuee whose name I can't remember — I never remember her complaining or scolding or burdening us with chores. After about a year, Harry returned home, and at the same time I went to boarding school. Uprooting children seemed normal

Harry polishing shoes on the doorstep of our New Brunswick home, 1954.

back then. The war meant thousands of children were uprooted, many not to relatives. I shared some of my years with a red-headed evacuee from England.

When we moved to Canada, in that first year in New Brunswick I worked at the Royal Bank and Harry worked at the pulp mill. He hated the smell and it seemed to get into his skin and hair. It was awful, like sulphur, but it never hindered him from finding a girlfriend. He bought a second-hand convertible and then he found the girl. When he decided to go into the Mounties, the

Formal picture of Harry as a Mountie.

Another formal photo of Harry as a Mountie.

family had moved to Montreal and Harry was dating the girl who would become his wife. Muriel was loyal to him while he went off to Regina for training. When he thought he might get posted way up north for years, he left the Mounties for the local Montreal police force and he and Muriel set up home in Montreal. He gave up the Mounties for the love of his life.

 I had long periods of living apart from my brother (geographically) when we were children and in our teens in Ireland, and then in Canada. When I lived in Montreal, he was in Regina; and when he lived in Montreal I lived in Saskatchewan and New York. We just moved in and out of each other's lives for brief visits. I missed a lot because of those separations, but I treasured the times I did have, because cancer took him from us in the prime of his life, on April 11, 1994. Despite his law and order career, he was a sweet, good-natured man, kind and helpful. Even as the cancer consumed him, his smile and caring touch touched us all. As I think back I remember him as a gentle, thoughtful preteen boy and into his late teens; he was that same sweet friend, brother, son in his adult years.

CHAPTER THIRTEEN

Miscellaneous Memories

- Shopping with Aunt Gladys for her wedding dress, and sitting with her years later when she was upset at her husband's spending so much time drinking in pubs with his pals.
- Riding in the back of an old model-T in Kinsale. There were primroses all over the banks.
- My love of newspapers, which is connected to my grandmother's reading of newspapers from the front to the back — except the sports section.
- I remember the gypsies and their beautiful caravans. You couldn't trust them not to steal — for example, your chickens — but they usually just kept to themselves.
- My mother's tomato story: During the food rationing of the war and the

Harry and I with Aunt Glady, Mother's sister, at our parent's farm.

early post-war years, even in the south of Ireland things were tight. On one occasion my mom was returning from Belfast. I don't know whether she had bought the tomatoes or if a friend had a hothouse, but she had a brown paper bag full of big, juicy tomatoes that she was bringing home from Belfast to Kinsale — the length of the whole island. It was a food treasure. When she got to Cork it was well on into the evening and with no bus connection, and no phones, she decided to walk along the highway and thumb a lift. It was very safe to do so, in those days, but it was about seventeen miles of highway. She walked and walked, but there was little traffic. Eventually she took her shoes off and carried them. At one point she looked back and saw that her tomatoes had been falling through the bag and she only had three or four left — they were all along the highway, red blob after red blob. She turned around, despite aching feet, to salvage what she could.

- I never felt unsafe as a child because police patrolled on their bicycles and would stop and chat and you got to know them. They would always tell you, "Watch for a car." There weren't that many cars.
- Old and beautiful pens — that had a lever and the ink got sucked in or squirted out as required — not ball point pens like there are now
- Family will always remember Mother's rose garden in Montreal. The roses were so spectacular that she received an invitation to Buckingham Palace with a bunch of rose growers, to meet the Queen in her rose garden. That was the year

Mother was known for growing beautiful roses, so I love this picture of her with the roses on her left and on her right. This was taken when she lived on Beatty Avenue in Montreal.

they named the Centennial Rose — 1967.

- When we write about our lives, it's neither lying nor truth telling. I read that somewhere; I really like that — it's so true. Keeping some memories and discarding others — some things you can't tell because it will harm others who are still alive.

- Going to the well for drinking water. Dipping the bucket into clear, clear water in a well whose wall was all stoned in. The taste of a cup of that fresh water was amazing.

- When the shuttle took off in the late 1970s I was living in Ottawa. I knew the approximate time it would go over our house. I heard a noise and I rushed to the door, opened the sliding glass door — and crashed into the screen. I missed the drama, and all I got was a scratched nose.

- On the Miramichi River: In the old cemetery behind our house, at night the fireflies would come out. We had never seen fireflies before. At first it was spooky! We saw these lights around the tombstones. We had a Mountie friend who used his bicycle a lot. He would come as far as the cemetery and then lie with his head on one of the tombstones, having his afternoon nap.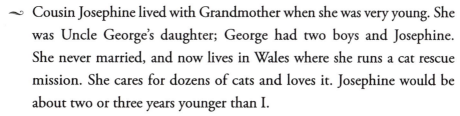

- Cousin Josephine lived with Grandmother when she was very young. She was Uncle George's daughter; George had two boys and Josephine. She never married, and now lives in Wales where she runs a cat rescue mission. She cares for dozens of cats and loves it. Josephine would be about two or three years younger than I.

- Fascination with rainbows: There were lots of double rainbows in Ireland. I used to see many and now they are lost in the smog. I love that song, "Somewhere over the rainbow."

- White bread: That was the greatest gift to humankind when it first came!

- My grandmother and Uncle Freddie loved dogs. Veany and Topsy were the two I remember well.

- Dating a blind boy: When I was a student at McGill doing my Bachelor of Divinity — Our first date was to a movie; I learned so much from him ... especially about the wisdom of listening well. He would take two buses to come and pick me up to go out.

- Grandmother and her always-available bottle of brandy — she said it was for health reasons. I never saw her drink it, but the levels always changed. She lived into her nineties — healthy and on her own. My mom did too. Grandmother had a pump organ *and* a piano — very unusual for a modest widow in a country house. She was very adamant that I ride my bike many country miles to piano lessons, hail, rain or shine.
- The primroses and the lilacs and the bluebells in the spring. There was a forest that was part of a huge estate; bluebells were so thick it was like walking on grass.
- One of my favourite musicians was Marion Anderson. I had all her records and loved to hear her sing "He's got the whole world in his hands." I also adored Van Kliburn, who was a young, classical pianist with so much talent.
- My son Andrew has always been incredibly thoughtful. I had thyroid surgery years ago at Wellesley Hospital in Toronto. I remember walking from the hospital to the train on a hot day wearing nylon panty hose and dressy shoes, and, when I got to the station, the blood was running out of the back of my heels. I was wounded top and bottom. Andrew soon came home and spent some treasured time with me. He has never failed to be supportive when I need him.

Naomi and Andrew — searching for googies!

- Naomi came into her new family at eight weeks old. Her dad and I were prepared for a new way of living. She was such an easy child to parent. She slept through the night, even as a small baby — unbelievable — even on the first night. Not fussy in the daytime — How could one not love her? Her maternal grandmother, my mother, thought adoption was not acceptable, but when we placed Naomi in her grandmother's arms, all that fell away and the two became lifelong friends. That beautiful baby became the best modelling of good parenting with her own children, Molly and Liam. It was just in her genes because I made lots of mistakes. One of the great mysteries of

Naomi frequently slept fallen forward like this.

Elizabeth with the children.

life — that easy child became a rebellious teen, but we all survived those years and she went on to be a good student and thrive in her chosen career of social work and as a model mom to Liam and Molly.

"Without memory, there is no healing.
Without forgiveness, there is no future."
— BISHOP TUTU

"All of us have failed to match our dreams of perfection.
I rate us on the basis of our splendid failure to do the impossible."
— WILLIAM FAULKNER

I wouldn't change any of my life, even the pain-filled parts, for the darkest times were tunnels through immovable mountains to bright new places. It's been a good ride, as I have attempted to pull together the years that have been given me, and, while I'm aware that my story is probably riddled with inaccuracies, it's still my story.

— ELIZABETH

God Bless the Moon and God Bless Me.

Genealogy Reports
for the Descendents

Genealogy Report for the Descendents of Faulkner

Generation 1

1. **Faulkner**-1.

    Faulkner and unknown spouse married. They had the following children:

    2. i. **Robert (Bobbie) Faulkner**. He died about 1942 in Castlegore, Co Tyrone, Northern Ireland. He married Dorien McAfee in Ireland.

    ii. **Margaret Faulkner**. She died in Aughnahoo, Co Tyrone, Northern Ireland.

    Notes for Margaret Faulkner:
    General Notes:
    Maggie was never married and died in housefire with her brother, Samuel.

    iii. **Samuel Faulkner**. He died in Aughnahoo, Co Tyrone, Northern Ireland.

    Notes for Samuel Faulkner:
    General Notes:
    Samuel died in a housefire with his sister, Margaret (Maggie).
    Samuel was never married.

Generation 2

2. **Robert (Bobbie) Faulkner**-2 (Father-1). He died about 1942 in Castlegore, Co Tyrone, Northern Ireland.

    Dorien McAfee daughter of Johnston McAfee and Elizabeth Jane (Lizzie) Echlin was born on 11 Aug 1911 in Quetta, India (now Pakistan). She died on 18 Feb 2007 in Kitchener, Ontario, Canada.

    Notes for Dorien McAfee:
    General Notes:
    Moved to Ireland as a small child, she was the oldest of her siblings and had 1 sister and two brothers.

    Robert (Bobbie) Faulkner and Dorien McAfee were married in Ireland. They had the following children:

Genealogy Report for the Descendents of Faulkner

Generation 2 (con't)

3. i. **Margaret Elizabeth (Betty) Faulkner** was born on 09 Sep 1933 in Castlegore, Co Tyrone, Northern Ireland (at home). She married Petrus (Peter) Praamsma on 28 Oct 1967 in Verdun United Church, Verdon, Quebec (officiated by Rev Rex Dolan and Rev Aelfryn Jones).

4. ii. **Robert Henry (Harry) Faulkner** was born on 04 May 1936 in Castlegore, Co Tyrone, Northern Ireland. He married Muriel Anne Whitlock on 02 Jun 1962 in Verdun, Quebec, Canada. He died on 11 Apr 1994.

Generation 3

3. **Margaret Elizabeth (Betty) Faulkner**-3 (Robert (Bobbie)-2, Father-1) was born on 09 Sep 1933 in Castlegore, Co Tyrone, Northern Ireland (at home).

Petrus (Peter) Praamsma was born in Aug 1939 in Joure, Holland.

Petrus (Peter) Praamsma and Margaret Elizabeth (Betty) Faulkner were married on 28 Oct 1967 in Verdun United Church, Verdon, Quebec (officiated by Rev Rex Dolan and Rev Aelfryn Jones). They had the following children:

5. i. **Naomi Dorien Praamsma** was born on 04 Jul 1968 in Montreal, Quebec, Canada (Adopted). She married John Henderson in 1993 in Ottawa, Ontario, Canada.

   ii. **Andrew Peter Praamsma** was born on 16 Jun 1971 in Civic Hospital, Ottawa, Ontario, Canada.

4. **Robert Henry (Harry) Faulkner**-3 (Robert (Bobbie)-2, Father-1) was born on 04 May 1936 in Castlegore, Co Tyrone, Northern Ireland. He died on 11 Apr 1994.

Muriel Anne Whitlock was born on 29 Nov 1939. She died on 26 Oct 2008.

Robert Henry (Harry) Faulkner and Muriel Anne Whitlock were married on 02 Jun 1962 in Verdun, Quebec, Canada. They had the following children:

6. i. **Lynne Marie Faulkner** was born on 23 Jan 1964. She married Mark John Lucas on 07 Aug 1982 in Port Elgin, Ontario, Canada.

Genealogy Report for the Descendents of Faulkner

Generation 3 (con't)

7.   ii.   **Anne Elizabeth Faulkner** was born on 04 Aug 1967 in Montreal, Quebec, Canada.

Doreen McIntosh was born on 28 Aug 1928.

Notes for Doreen McIntosh:
General Notes:
McIntosh was Doreen's name from a previous marriage, not her maiden name.

Robert Henry (Harry) Faulkner and Doreen McIntosh married. They had no children.

Generation 4

5.   **Naomi Dorien Praamsma**-4 (Margaret Elizabeth (Betty)-3, Robert (Bobbie)-2, Father-1) was born on 04 Jul 1968 in Montreal, Quebec, Canada (Adopted).

John Henderson.

John Henderson and Naomi Dorien Praamsma were married in 1993 in Ottawa, Ontario, Canada. They had the following children:

    i.   **Liam Alexander Henderson** was born on 13 Feb 1995 in Ottawa, Ontario, Canada.

    ii.   **Molly Elizabeth Henderson** was born on 05 Sep 1997 in Ottawa, Ontario, Canada.

6.   **Lynne Marie Faulkner**-4 (Robert Henry (Harry)-3, Robert (Bobbie)-2, Father-1) was born on 23 Jan 1964.

Mark John Lucas was born on 15 Apr 1960.

Mark John Lucas and Lynne Marie Faulkner were married on 07 Aug 1982 in Port Elgin, Ontario, Canada. They had the following children:

    i.   **Matthew Mark Lucas** was born on 07 Feb 1985.

Generation 4 (con't)

        ii.   **Pamela Lynne Lucas** was born on 19 Jun 1986.

        iii.   **Bradley Robert Allan Lucas** was born on 22 Sep 1988.

7.   **Anne Elizabeth Faulkner**-4 (Robert Henry (Harry)-3, Robert (Bobbie)-2, Father-1) was born on 04 Aug 1967 in Montreal, Quebec, Canada.

Anne Elizabeth Faulkner and unknown spouse married. They had the following children:

        i.   **Branden** was born on 26 Apr 1988.

        ii.   **Cameron** was born on 22 Feb 1990.

        iii.   **Melanie Lynne** was born on 18 Jun 1992.

        iv.   **Bethany Anne** was born on 15 Jan 1999.

Genealogy Report for the Descendents of Johnston McAfee

Generation 1

1. **Johnston McAfee**-1. He died on 03 Jan 1917 in Salonika, Greece (Died on way home from WWI)[1].

   Notes for Johnston McAfee:
   General Notes:
   Johnston served during WWI in the Royal Irish Fusiliers 2nd Battalion. He was the Company Quarter Master Sergeant. The battalion would have 297 deaths during the war (http://www.northeastmedals.co.uk/british_regiment/irish/royal_irish_fusiliers.htm : 15 June 2011). There would be at most about 1000 men in a battalion but in reality having 600 men was more probable (http://battlefields1418.50megs.com/battalion.htm : 15 June 2011).

   He would serve the 1914-1915 campaign in Egypt. He would receive 3 medals; the Victory, British and Service Star medals.

   Transferred with the British Army to India (now Pakistan) in 1911. He was killed on his way home from WW1 in 3 January 1917 Salonika, Greece.

   Elizabeth Jane (Lizzie) Echlin was born in Co. Wicklow, Southern Ireland.

   Notes for Elizabeth Jane (Lizzie) Echlin:
   General Notes:
   Moved to India in 1911 with Johnston McAfee.
   The first born died at a few months old and his grave was 'eaten up' in a subsequent earthquake (a life long pain in grandmothers heart).
   Their first surviving child, Dorien, was born in Quette, India, the oldest of five children.
   Doriens father, my "never knew" grandfather was killed when his homecoming ship hit a mine. Her brother James (Jimmy) used to visit Lizzie on his bike. Lizzie moved to Northern Ireland to be close to Jimmy when she was widowed.

   Johnston McAfee and Elizabeth Jane (Lizzie) Echlin married. They had the following children:

   2. i. **Dorien McAfee** was born on 11 Aug 1911 in Ouetta, India (now Pakistan). She died on 18 Feb 2007 in Kitchener, Ontario, Canada. She married Robert (Bobbie) Faulkner in Ireland.

   3. ii. **Gladys McAfee**.

      iii. **Frederick (Freddie) McAfee**.

      iv. **George (Georgie) McAfee**.

Genealogy Report for the Descendents of Johnston McAfee

Generation 2

2. **Dorien McAfee**-2 (Johnston-1) was born on 11 Aug 1911 in Ouetta, India (now Pakistan). She died on 18 Feb 2007 in Kitchener, Ontario, Canada.

   Notes for Dorien McAfee:
   General Notes:
   Moved to Ireland as a small child, she was the oldest of her siblings and had 1 sister and two brothers.

   Robert (Bobbie) Faulkner son of Faulkner. He died about 1942 in Castlegore, Co Tyrone, Northern Ireland.

   Robert (Bobbie) Faulkner and Dorien McAfee were married in Ireland. They had the following children:

   4. i. **Margaret Elizabeth (Betty) Faulkner** was born on 09 Sep 1933 in Castlegore, Co Tyrone, Northern Ireland (at home). She married Petrus (Peter) Praamsma on 28 Oct 1967 in Verdun United Church, Verdon, Quebec (officiated by Rev Rex Dolan and Rev Aelfryn Jones).

   5. ii. **Robert Henry (Harry) Faulkner** was born on 04 May 1936 in Castlegore, Co Tyrone, Northern Ireland. He married Muriel Anne Whitlock on 02 Jun 1962 in Verdun, Quebec, Canada. He died on 11 Apr 1994.

   Aelfryn Ernest Jones was born in 1909 in Wales. He died in 1990 in Kitchener, Ontario, Canada.

   Notes for Aelfryn Ernest Jones:
   General Notes:
   Lived in Sommerset, England in his early years. Moved to Northern Ireland.

   Aelfryn Ernest Jones and Dorien McAfee were married in 1944. They had no children.

3. **Gladys McAfee**-2 (Johnston-1).

   Herbert Scott.

   Herbert Scott and Gladys McAfee married. They had the following children:

   i. **Valerie Scott**.

   ii. **Noleen Scott**.

Genealogy Report for the Descendents of Johnston McAfee

Generation 3

4. **Margaret Elizabeth (Betty) Faulkner**-3 (Dorien-2, Johnston-1) was born on 09 Sep 1933 in Castlegore, Co Tyrone, Northern Ireland (at home).

   Petrus (Peter) Praamsma was born in Aug 1939 in Joure, Holland.

   Petrus (Peter) Praamsma and Margaret Elizabeth (Betty) Faulkner were married on 28 Oct 1967 in Verdun United Church, Verdon, Quebec (officiated by Rev Rex Dolan and Rev Aelfryn Jones). They had the following children:

   6.   i.   **Naomi Dorien Praamsma** was born on 04 Jul 1968 in Montreal, Quebec, Canada (Adopted). She married John Henderson in 1993 in Ottawa, Ontario, Canada.

        ii. **Andrew Peter Praamsma** was born on 16 Jun 1971 in Civic Hospital, Ottawa, Ontario, Canada.

5. **Robert Henry (Harry) Faulkner**-3 (Dorien-2, Johnston-1) was born on 04 May 1936 in Castlegore, Co Tyrone, Northern Ireland. He died on 11 Apr 1994.

   Muriel Anne Whitlock was born on 29 Nov 1939. She died on 26 Oct 2008.

   Robert Henry (Harry) Faulkner and Muriel Anne Whitlock were married on 02 Jun 1962 in Verdun, Quebec, Canada. They had the following children:

   7.   i.   **Lynne Marie Faulkner** was born on 23 Jan 1964. She married Mark John Lucas on 07 Aug 1982 in Port Elgin, Ontario, Canada.

   8.   ii. **Anne Elizabeth Faulkner** was born on 04 Aug 1967 in Montreal, Quebec, Canada.

   Doreen McIntosh was born on 28 Aug 1928.

   Notes for Doreen McIntosh:
   General Notes:
   McIntosh was Doreen's name from a previous marriage, not her maiden name.

   Robert Henry (Harry) Faulkner and Doreen McIntosh married. They had no children.

Generation 4

6. **Naomi Dorien Praamsma**-4 (Margaret Elizabeth (Betty)-3, Dorien-2, Johnston-1) was born on 04 Jul 1968 in Montreal, Quebec, Canada (Adopted).

Genealogy Report for the Descendents of Johnston McAfee

Generation 4 (con't)

John Henderson.

John Henderson and Naomi Dorien Praamsma were married in 1993 in Ottawa, Ontario, Canada. They had the following children:

    i.   **Liam Alexander Henderson** was born on 13 Feb 1995 in Ottawa, Ontario, Canada.

    ii.   **Molly Elizabeth Henderson** was born on 05 Sep 1997 in Ottawa, Ontario, Canada.

7. **Lynne Marie Faulkner**-4 (Robert Henry (Harry)-3, Dorien-2, Johnston-1) was born on 23 Jan 1964.

Mark John Lucas was born on 15 Apr 1960.

Mark John Lucas and Lynne Marie Faulkner were married on 07 Aug 1982 in Port Elgin, Ontario, Canada. They had the following children:

    i.   **Matthew Mark Lucas** was born on 07 Feb 1985.

    ii.   **Pamela Lynne Lucas** was born on 19 Jun 1986.

    iii.   **Bradley Robert Allan Lucas** was born on 22 Sep 1988.

8. **Anne Elizabeth Faulkner**-4 (Robert Henry (Harry)-3, Dorien-2, Johnston-1) was born on 04 Aug 1967 in Montreal, Quebec, Canada.

Anne Elizabeth Faulkner and unknown spouse married. They had the following children:

    i.   **Branden** was born on 26 Apr 1988.

    ii.   **Cameron** was born on 22 Feb 1990.

    iii.   **Melanie Lynne** was born on 18 Jun 1992.

    iv.   **Bethany Anne** was born on 15 Jan 1999.

Sources

1   The Comittee of the Irish National War Memorial, comp. Ireland`s Memorial Records 1914-1918. 8 volumes. Dublin: Maunsel and Roberts, 1923.